Hugh O'Brien

## Inaugural Address of Hugh O'Brien

Mayor of Boston, before the City Council, January 4, 1886

Hugh O'Brien

**Inaugural Address of Hugh O'Brien**
*Mayor of Boston, before the City Council, January 4, 1886*

ISBN/EAN: 9783337302047

Printed in Europe, USA, Canada, Australia, Japan

Cover: Foto ©Suzi / pixelio.de

More available books at **www.hansebooks.com**

# INAUGURAL ADDRESS

OF

# HUGH O'BRIEN,

MAYOR OF BOSTON,

BEFORE

## THE CITY COUNCIL,

JANUARY 4, 1886.

BOSTON:
ROCKWELL AND CHURCHILL, CITY PRINTERS,
No. 39 Arch Street.
1886.

# CITY OF BOSTON.

In Board of Aldermen, Jan. 7, 1886.

*Ordered*, That His Honor the Mayor be requested to furnish a copy of his Inaugural Address, and that the same be printed as a City Document, and in the volume of Proceedings of the City Council.

Passed in Common Council, January 4, 1886. Came up for concurrence. Concurred. Approved by the Mayor, January 8, 1886.

A true copy.

Attest :

JOHN T. PRIEST,
*Assistant City Clerk.*

# ADDRESS.

*Gentlemen of the City Council: —*

To-day we assemble to take charge of an important trust, placed in our hands by our fellow-citizens. On our joint action, in a great degree, the growth and prosperity of the city depend. Let peace and harmony prevail in our councils. Let us not forget that our city stands at the head of municipal governments. The reputation of our public school system must be maintained. The health of the city must be preserved. Our business and manufacturing industries must be promoted and encouraged. We must have efficient fire and police departments. We want good streets, good sewerage, and pure water. Our poor, our insane, and our criminals must be taken care of and provided for. You will be called upon during the year to consider questions involving all these interests, requiring large expenditures of money, and every appropriation should be closely scrutinized and fully considered. As the legislative branch it is your duty to furnish the means, and as the executive branch it is my duty to see that what money you appropriate is properly, economically, and faithfully expended.

The new departure will be in full force during the year, and if our work is done as it ought to be done, free from all selfish purposes, the year 1886 will be a memorable one in our municipal history. The fact that aldermen are elected by districts and councilmen by wards should have no weight with you. The entire city is under your charge, and every district and every ward should be fairly and equitably dealt with. I have no hesitation in saying here, what I have said many times before, that aldermanic districts are no improvement on our old municipal system of electing aldermen at large. If the members of the Common Council look only after the interests of the wards they represent, and the aldermen after their districts, we can scarcely expect that loyalty to all sections of the city which is so desirable in a city government.

The new City Charter places great responsibility on the Mayor of Boston. The faithful performance of his duty requires good judgment, close attention to business, a thorough knowledge of the work, and courage and determination in its performance. If the Mayor stops waste and

extravagance he makes determined and unscrupulous enemies of men whose sole object is
public plunder, and who do not hesitate to resort
to any means to accomplish their ends. Regardless of threats, regardless sometimes of adverse
criticism from parties who do not understand the
true facts, I have given no quarter the last year
to any who have abused the trusts confided to
them, and with such an emphatic indorsement
from my fellow-citizens I feel encouraged to go
on with the work. Political tricksters, who have
merely some selfish purpose to gratify, will receive
no countenance from me no matter what party
they may be identified with for the time being.
It is by yielding to these men, on account of
the few votes that they control, that municipal
governments, in all the large cities of the country,
have become a synonyme for waste and extravagance and corruption. This is strong language,
but I know that every word of it is true. If
political parties put unscrupulous men to the
front they ought to be voted down. If political
parties make combinations with men whose morality
and integrity are questionable, such combinations
should be discouraged and discountenanced by
every good citizen. If no quarter is given to
men who have no moral principle behind them,

who connect themselves with leading parties merely for plunder, they will soon be stamped out, and the business of the city will be conducted like any other large corporation, on business principles. I believe that the new charter will accomplish this work, if faithfully administered.

This charter went into operation on the 26th of last June. It cannot be said to have had a fair trial as yet. Most of the heads of departments have cheerfully conformed to the new order of things, and hold more independent positions than under the old charter, when directed and controlled by committees. They are required to do all work in a substantial and economical manner, and live within the limits of their appropriations. As long as they do this *their tenure of office should be secure.* The departments are no longer political machines, but must be run, like any other corporation in the city, solely on business principles.

I repeat, that the City Charter has hardly had a fair trial during the past six months, because an unusual percentage of last year's appropriation was placed, early in the financial year, by contract or otherwise, before it went into operation. This was rather embarrassing to commence with, but the difficulty has been met and overcome. I know that a large sum of money has already been saved.

Contracts have been given to the lowest responsible bidders in all instances, and supplies have been purchased at the lowest market rates. I might make a comparison with previous years, but it is sufficient to say that, with a tax-rate of $12.80 per $1,000, all necessary work has been performed. The coming year the charter will have full force, and, if faithful and honest work is done in the departments, the results cannot help being a substantial gain to the city. I cannot recommend any alteration or change at present. If defects exist, time will develop them more fully. It places power in the hands of the Mayor to hold even the City Council in check, if that body is derelict in the performance of their duty, and, if the Mayor is a true Bostonian, he will not hesitate to take the responsibility.

The following table shows the amount of the transfers made by order of the City Council during the past ten years, the amount added to the regular appropriations, and the percentage of these additions to the total of transfers: —

| Year. | Total of Transfers. | Transfers to Regular Appropriations. | Percentage. |
|---|---|---|---|
| 1875–76 . . | $714,880 97 | $255,459 40 | 35.7 |
| 1876–77 | 418,398 54 | 129,298 24 | 30.9 |
| 1877–78 . . | 211,167 50 | 121,823 02 | 58. |
| 1878–79 . . | 171,404 32 | 135,484 75 | 71.5 |
| 1879–80 . . | 342,187 07 | 241,597 81 | 70.6 |
| 1880–81 . . | 270,314 35 | 192,174 25 | 71. |
| 1881–82 . . | 229,659 07 | 165,124 38 | 71.9 |
| 1882–83 . . | 261,010 11 | 158,803 08 | 60.8 |
| 1883–84 . . | 279,497 96 | 127,413 42 | 45.8 |
| 1884–85 . | 282,266 87 | 143,010 71 | 50.7 |

## THE CITY DEBT.

Gross funded debt, Dec. 31, 1884 . . . $42,981,934 91
Add funded debt issued in 1885 . . . 1,742,700 00

$44,724,634 91
Deduct funded debt paid in 1885 . . . 1,307,689 07

Gross debt, Dec. 31, 1885 . . . . $43,416,945 84
Sinking-funds, Dec. 31, 1884 . $17,845,950 12
Receipts during 1885 . . 1,861,633 64

$19,707,583 76
Payments during 1885 . 1,320,439 45

$18,387,144 31
Difference in settlement of Den-
nie deficit . . . . 39,234 38

*Amounts carried forward,*   $18,347,909 93 $43,416,945 84

| | | |
|---|---|---|
| *Amounts brought forward,* | $18,347,909 93 | $43,416,945 84 |
| Bonds and mortgages, the payments of which are pledged to the payment of debt . | 369,021 62 | |
| Total redemption means, Dec. 31, 1885. . | | 18,716,931 55 |
| Net debt, Dec. 31, 1885 . . . . . | | $24,700,014 29 |

| | |
|---|---|
| Gross debt, Dec. 31, 1885 . . . | $43,416,945 84 |
| Gross debt, Dec. 31, 1884 . . . . | 42,981,934 91 |
| Increase . . . . . . . | $435,010 93 |

| | |
|---|---|
| Net debt, Dec. 31, 1884. . . . . | $24,766,064 27 |
| Net debt, Dec. 31, 1885 . . . . . | 24,700,014 29 |
| Decrease . . . . . . . | $66,049 98 |

| | |
|---|---|
| City debt, including balance of debts assumed by acts of annexation . . . . . | $29,367,471 86 |
| Cochituate Water debt . . . . | 13,210,473 98 |
| Mystic Water debt . . . . . . | 839,000 00 |
| | $43,416,945 84 |

Loans authorized, but not issued, by City Council of 1883 : —

| | |
|---|---|
| Library Building, Dartmouth st. and St. James ave. . . . . . . . . | $440,000 00 |
| *Amount carried forward,* | $440,000 00 |

| | | |
|---|---:|---:|
| *Amount brought forward,* | | $440,000 00 |

By City Council of 1884 : —

| | | |
|---|---:|---:|
| Additional supply of water . | $150,000 00 | |
| High-service . . | 549,000 00 | |
| | | 699,000 00 |

By City Council of 1885 : —

| | | |
|---|---:|---:|
| Improved Sewerage . . | $100,000 00 | |
| Extension of mains, etc. . | 100,000 00 | |
| Home for Paupers . . . | 80,000 00 | |
| | | 280,000 00 |
| | | $1,419,000 00 |

At the present time the assumed debts remaining unpaid are, on account of : —

| | | | |
|---|---:|---:|---:|
| Charlestown city . . . . | $1,002,000 00, | bearing | 6% |
| Mystic water . . $716,000 00 | | " | 6% |
| " " . 108,000 00 | | " | 5% |
| " " . 15,000 00 | | " | 4% |
| | 839,000 00 | | |
| | $1,841,000 00 | | |
| West Roxbury . . . . | 140,000 00 | " | 7% |
| | $1,981,000 00 | | |

The net debt for eleven years compares as follows : —

| | |
|---|---:|
| December 31, 1885 . . . . | . $24,700,014 29 |
| December 31, 1884 . . . . | . 24,766,064 27 |
| December 31, 1883 . . | . 25,311,635 52 |

| | |
|---|---|
| December 31, 1882 | . $24,381,025 02 |
| December 31, 1881 | . 24,248,046 60 |
| December 31, 1880 | . 26,658,456 41 |
| December 31, 1879 | . 26,097,783 05 |
| December 31, 1878 | . 26,184,171 42 |
| December 31, 1877 | . 26,855,464 94 |
| December 31, 1876 | . 28,376,362 24 |
| December 31, 1875 | . 28,752,635 02 |

It will be seen that the net debt is now about $4,000,000 less than in 1875, and that since that date important and expensive public improvements have been carried on, notably : improved sewerage, the Sudbury-river water supply, including a new conduit, the establishment of parks, besides large expenditures for construction. This speaks well for the financial condition of the city.

### TAXATION. — FINANCE.

The tax levy last year was made up as follows: —

| | |
|---|---|
| Appropriated | $10,608,100 |
| Estimated income | 2,804,550 |
| | $7,803,550 |
| Add 4 per cent. | 312,142 |
| Total tax levy | $8,115,692 |

The following is an estimate for the coming
year, based on last year's income, interest, and
sinking-fund requirements: —

| | |
|---|---:|
| Outside limit of appropriation . . . | $10,713,751 |
| Estimated income . . . . | 2,804,550 |
| | $7,907,201 |
| Add 4 per cent. . . . . . | 316,368 |
| Probable tax levy . . . | $8,225,569 |

These figures show that the City Government
will have to be run economically the coming
year to keep within the limit, and that the expenses of departments must be cut down to the
lowest possible figures. The highest amount that
can be taxed in the next year cannot now be
definitely determined, because of the lack of an
estimate of income. An estimate of the receipts
from taxation and income on investments of the
sinking-funds, exclusive of water-debt funds, during 1886, is $1,350,000.

By Chapter 178, Acts of 1885, the limit of taxation, exclusive of State tax and the requirements of the debt, was fixed at $9, on a basis
of the average valuation for *five years,* while, by
Chapter 312, Acts of 1885, the limit for other cities

was fixed at $12, on a basis of the average valuation for *three years*. Another item in favor of the outside cities was the exemption of the county tax, which, with Boston for the last year, was $375,000, and this, less estimate of county income, was 27 cents of the tax-rate of $12.80 of the present year. Notwithstanding all this special legislation, so far as Boston is concerned, I am satisfied our municipal work can be done within the limit.

The valuation of the city, the new property built up, and the tax-rate, since January, 1874, has been as follows: —

| Year. | Assessors' Valuation. | Estimated Value of New Buildings. | Tax-Rate. |
|---|---|---|---|
| 1874 | $798,755,050 | $16,797,735 | $15.60 |
| 1875 | 793,961,895 | 10,546,520 | 13.70 |
| 1876 | 748,996,210 | 6,727,130 | 12.70 |
| 1877 | 686,840,586 | 5,332,365 | 13.10 |
| 1878 | 630,446,866 | 3,447,655 | 12.80 |
| 1879 | 613,322,691 | 2,266,084 | 12.50 |
| 1880 | 639,462,495 | 1,964,852 | 15.20 |
| 1881 | 665,554,597 | 2,208,496 | 13.90 |
| 1882 | 672,497,961 | 7,311,918 | 15.10 |
| 1883 | 682,432,671 | 7,535,383 | 14.50 |
| 1884 | 682,648,000 | 8,298,970 | 17.00 |
| 1885 | 685,404,600 | 12,963,630 | 12.80 |

Taxation now has a limit; the indebtedness of the city has a limit, and the citizens of Boston have an assurance that in no year in the future can taxation be unreasonable or our indebtedness exceed two per cent. on valuation. This, I am confident, gives us an ample margin. The law limiting indebtedness was imperfect without a similar law limiting taxation. With these safeguards the financial condition of the city is beyond question now or in the future. It was very gratifying to know that no other city in the Commonwealth could carry on its municipal work on so small a margin as the city of Boston. This was quite manifest during the discussion in the Legislature last year. In New York the limit of indebtedness is ten per cent. on the assessed valuation of real estate subject to taxation, and with this limit that city finds it difficult to carry on the large improvements now in progress.

Some years ago, when I had the honor to call attention to the necessity of a law limiting taxation in the Board of Aldermen, and offered an order to petition the Legislature for such a law, it was voted down almost unanimously; but I am now satisfied that every large city in the country will be compelled to follow the example

of Boston, and ask for similar laws to check
municipal taxation and municipal indebtedness.
These checks, however, do not prevent waste or
extravagance. No matter how large or small our
annual appropriation may be, it can be wasted
by incompetent or unscrupulous heads of departments, unless checked by the Mayor with all the
force and power conferred upon him by the new
charter.

I shall always consider it a great honor that
a Republican Legislature intrusted me with such
great power. I have also received excellent advice
and encouragement, during the year, not only from
the press, but from some of our best citizens and
largest tax-payers, and I trust that this advice
and support will be continued during the coming
year. I have endeavored to enforce the law dis-
creetly and firmly.

Some sections of our city are growing rapidly,
notably the Back Bay district, Dorchester, and
West Roxbury, and require large expenditures
for streets and sewers. When capitalists are
ready to plant large sums of money in improvements, adding very materially to our taxable
property, it is the duty of the city to encourage
them by providing good streets, sewerage, water,
and other improvements that are under our charge.

For every dollar judiciously expended in this way the city treasury is benefited by an increased amount of taxable property. Some of the improvements demanded are large and costly, and would be embarrassing if placed in the tax levy. These improvements should be commenced on some systematic plan, and not as a temporary expedient. n the past, sewers have been built without giving due consideration to the subject, and the consequence has been that we have been creating nuisances instead of remedying them. To meet this demand it has been found necessary to do some of this work by a loan rather than to check building operations and the growth of the city for the time being. It is wise policy to pay as we go for all necessary improvements; but when they are costly and permanent there is no good reason why the tax-payers of to-day should pay for the entire work. It should be remembered, also, that our limit of indebtedness is a check and safeguard on these loans. If we could pay off our debts without incurring new loans, and, at the same time, carry on all the improvements required for a city that is growing rapidly, our financial condition would be perfect. I am satisfied, however, that, notwithstanding all the improvements in contemplation, there will be a material reduction in our debt during the next ten years.

I am aware that the delay in widening Boylston street has already interfered with building operations. It has also prevented us from building a police-station and an engine-house, so necessary for the safety of that section, for which an appropriation has already been made. Now that the money has been obtained the work on the Boylston-street extension, and also the Beacon-street extension, will be commenced in earnest as soon as the weather will permit. Humboldt avenue was laid out nearly three years ago, the owners of property contributing the land. The property on the line of that avenue has been assessed at a higher valuation, on account of the contemplated improvements, and the owners of property have been put to great distress because they could neither sell their land nor erect buildings until the city lived up to their agreement. Good reasons can be given for all the improvements contemplated in the loan passed at the close of the year, but the way in which it was engineered through the Council, and the amount of trading to obtain the necessary two-thirds vote, was, to say the least, highly objectionable.

The banks in the city of Boston, with the

exception of six, have paid the tax assessed by authority of the laws of this Commonwealth, for the year 1885, under protest, alleging that the tax assessed on them was not at the same rate assessed on similar moneyed capital. The total amount of bank tax received and paid by the Collector to the City Treasurer was $773,-478.40; of this sum, $720,723.20 was paid under protest; $35,685.52 received from those banks which made no protests, less commission for collecting, has been paid by the City Treasurer to the State, leaving due the State of Massachusetts $547,193.98 received with protests, which payment has been withholden from the State by the City Treasurer, under advice of the Corporation Counsel; and the State Treasurer, in consequence, withholds the payment to the city of the corporation tax, bank tax from other cities and towns, "the tax on vessels engaged in foreign trade," and a portion of the reimbursement of the amount paid by the city for State aid to soldiers, etc., in all about the same amount which the city withholds. It has prevented the settlement of the accounts between the treasurers of our city and the State. The counsel having in charge the suits of protest will, it is understood, press them for trial. Therefore, it will probably

be some time before the final decision of the same
will be reached. In the meantime the Legislature
of our State will undoubtedly, at its coming session, devise means by which the moneys can be
paid by the city, and the city receive the amount
due it from the State, and protection guaranteed
from loss if any money is recovered from the
city in the suits brought by the banks.

While on the subject of taxation I cannot help
again alluding to the taxation of our manufacturing and industrial pursuits. In my inaugural last
year I stated that "there are many manufacturers
whose salesrooms and warehouses are in Boston, but
who manufacture their goods in other places, for
the reason that not only are the tax-rates lower,
but they are also able to make arrangements with
the local assessors for a certain definite valuation
of their property. It would be more convenient
for them to manufacture their goods in Boston,
but the high rate, with the excessive valuation,
prevents. It is well worth considering whether it
would not be wise policy to revise the methods
of assessment so as to draw these manufacturers
into the city. . . . The extent of our de-
pendence on neighboring States for many articles
of large consumption can scarcely be realized.
If we could guarantee lower rates of taxation, and

a cheaper supply of water for manufacturing ur-
poses, I am satisfied it would build up our industrial
and manufacturing interests, and largely increase
the wealth of the city." I consider this a matter of
great importance, and the question should be agitated
until the necessary reforms are brought about.

The City Treasurer has so managed his department that he was enabled to meet all the
payments of the city of Boston during the year,
with the promptness which has always characterized its financial affairs, by borrowing the smallest
amount of temporary loan, in anticipation of the taxes,
since 1880, — viz., $1,300,000, — at the lowest rate
money has ever been borrowed by the city of Boston, the rate being two per cent. per annum. The
time for the principal portion of it was four months.

### THE COLLECTOR'S DEPARTMENT.

The Collector's department has done excellent
work during the year, and I feel that particular
attention ought to be called to it. The collection
of taxes shows a large increase in percentage
over any previous year for thirty-one years; but
what is most noticeable is the collection of sewer
assessments, amounting to $82,286.95, against
$13,198.41 last year. By a special message early
in the year I called attention to this matter, nd

it is gratifying to know that it produced such
good results. The collections for the previous
ten years were only $196,736.56. The collections
this year in nine months have been $82,286.95,
and before the close of the financial year the
amount may equal one-half the amount collected
the previous ten years. The assessments levied
in the ten years referred to were $539,795.48;
the amount collected $196,736.56, — leaving a
balance of $343,058.92 to account for. What
has become of this large sum? Has it been
abated? It appears to me a matter that ought
to be looked into and all the facts ascertained.

The assessments committed to the Collector for
the current financial year, beginning May 1,
1885, amount to $10,097,397.41.

Of this amount there has been collected to
December 1, 1885, $7,807,441.75, or 77$\frac{3}{10}$ per cent.;
abated, $84,643.76, or $\frac{9}{10}$ of 1 per cent.; and re-
mains uncollected, $2,205,311.90, or 21$\frac{8}{10}$ per cent.

This amount committed includes the State, City,
and County tax of 1885, $8,815,787.24, of which,
to December 19, 1885, $7,232,415.58 has been
collected; bank tax, $773,478.40, all of which has
been paid; and sewer assessments, $123,274.59,
of which, to December 19, 1885, $82,286.95 has
been collected. The percentage of taxes and

sewer assessments collected this year greatly exceeds that of any other year to the same time.

The total amount of collections for the eleven months, beginning January 1, 1885, and ending November 30, 1885, is $12,466,535.08, divided as follows: —

| | |
|---|---:|
| From Taxes | $9,375,116 57 |
| Cochituate Water-Works | 1,252,842 43 |
| Liquor Licenses | 507,595 00 |
| Mystic Water-Works | 281,834 86 |
| East Boston Ferries | 143,208 60 |
| Rents | 134,314 96 |
| Public Institutions | 105,270 15 |
| County of Suffolk | 97,575 65 |
| Sewer Department | 92,240 22 |
| Interest | 65,037 35 |
| Betterments | 54,532 68 |
| Health Department | 40,276 51 |
| Bonds | 40,221 51 |
| City Hospital | 32,600 29 |
| Street Department | 32,693 30 |
| School Instructors | 30,598 10 |
| Overseers of the Poor | 30,005 99 |
| All other sources | 150,570 91 |

The change in the ordinances transferring the entire labor of the collection of water-rates to the Collector's department will require an additional appropriation for extra clerk-hire. The additional expense is estimated at $2,000. This will be chargeable to the revenues from Cochituate and Mystic water-rates, and may be considered in the light of a transfer, and not as an additional expense. The work has formerly been done in the office of the Water Registrar.

The annual increase of business, the demands for the proper accommodation of the public, and care of the records and accounts, require a much larger room for this department. I do not see how this can at present be allowed, but I have taken the liberty of calling attention to the subject as among the most imperative prospective wants of the department.

*Sewers, — Assessed and Collected.*

| From May 1, | Assessed. | Collected. | To |
|---|---|---|---|
| 1875 | $123,388 77 | $32,472 04 | May 1, 1876 |
| 1876 | 101,983 60 | 33,172 49 | "      1877 |
| 1877 | 38,095 36 | 13,398 27 | "      1878 |
| 1878 | 33,575 79 | 12,375 91 | "      1879 |
| 1879 | 22,141 89 | 10,196 72 | "      1880 |
| 1880 | 42,986 60 | 18,692 23 | "      1881 |
| 1881 | 68,973 75 | 32,021 21 | "      1882 |
| 1882 | 65,677 21 | 30,075 31 | "      1883 |
| 1883 | 37,174 38 | 16,764 96 | "      1884 |
| 1884 | 23,761 09 | 13,198 41 | "      1885 |
| 1885 | 123.274 59 | 82,286 95 | Dec. 19, 1885 |
| | $681,033 03 | $294,654 50 | |

## PERCENTAGES OF TAXES COLLECTED.

The following table shows the percentages of taxes collected to Dec. 1 of each respective year, for the following years: —

| | | | |
|---|---|---|---|
| 1855, 56. | 1863, 52. | 1871, 39. | 1879, 69. |
| 1856, 55. | 1864, 50. | 1872, 56. | 1880, 72. |
| 1857, 45.5. | 1865, 54. | 1873, 58. | 1881, 73. |
| 1858, 54.5. | 1866, 55. | 1874, 52. | 1882, 71. |
| 1859, 54. | 1867, 50. | 1875, 59. | 1883, 72. |
| 1860, 46. | 1868, 49. | 1876, 63. | 1884, 73. |
| 1861, 47. | 1869, 43. | 1877, 64. | 1885, 76. |
| 1862, 51. | 1870, 42. | 1878, 69. | |

## THE GROWTH OF THE CITY.

The population of Boston in 1860 was 177,840; in 1870, including municipalities annexed, 292,499; in 1875, by State census, 341,912; in 1880, by United States census, 362,839; and in 1885, by State census, 390,406. The last census was a surprise to our citizens, and also to experts, who, from year to year, keep well informed on this subject. The work was done under the direction of Carroll D. Wright, Esq., a gentleman of large experience in collecting such information, and whose intelligence and ability cannot be questioned. This will stand as the official census for

the next ten years. Some months ago I called
the attention of the City Council to this matter,
and suggested that we had material connected
with the City Government to ascertain our population at a very small expense. I had an inter-
view with the Chairman of the Board of Police
Commissioners, and also with the chairman of the
Board of Assessors, and they agreed to under-
take the work if the City Council would appropriate $1,000 to print proper blanks and to pay
clerical assistance. These blanks would have been
placed in the hands of our large police force, and
in a very few days the facts could be collected,
and then the clerical force in the assessors'
department would aggregate the returns. I believe
that this would be an easy and economical way
of obtaining the population of the city at inter-
vals, apart from any State or United States census.
It would not interfere with the regular duties of
the police, and would be desirable information to
obtain. The last City Council, however, refused
to appropriate the $1,000 asked for. I still believe
the work ought to be done, and recommend it to
your favorable consideration. The population of
our city has been estimated as high as 425,000,
or near 35,000 more than the recent official
census.

## SURVEY OF VACANT LANDS.

The growth of the city also calls my attention to another important matter. In my inaugural address of last year I stated that there were large tracts of vacant land in the outlying districts not yet improved, and recommended that a survey be made and a comprehensive plan of prospective streets be adopted for those districts. If found necessary, additional legislation should be obtained to authorize the city to carry out such an improvement. Although no special survey has been made for this purpose during the year, one step in furtherance of it has been taken in the right direction. Plans have been prepared by the City Surveyor showing several proposed systems of streets through vacant land in the suburban districts, which plans are on file in the Surveyor's office, where they may be examined by parties interested. These plans are intended only to be preliminary to more accurate ones which will follow, and are subject, of course, to modification from time to time, as circumstances shall warrant. They have been drawn for the purpose of enabling the city and the owners of lands to coöperate in laying out a systematic plan of streets. It is hoped that the land-own-

ers will see it for their interest to meet the city
fairly in so important an improvement, otherwise
it may be necessary to ask for additional legislation to enable the city to carry out such an
improved system of streets.

## VACANCIES IN DEPARTMENTS.

One of the most difficult and perplexing duties
the Mayor has to perform is the selection of
proper heads of departments to fill vacancies
caused by dismissal, resignation, or death. A
vacancy no sooner occurs than large numbers
apply for the position, some of them entirely
incompetent. They are indorsed by numerous
friends, and the Mayor has no peace until the
vacancy is filled. I have offered positions to men
who have had all the requisite business qualifi-
cations and experience for the work, but have
found it a very difficult matter to obtain their
services. The risk of confirmation is also a bar
against acceptance. Such men generally do better
in business outside of city employment. The
salaries paid city officials will not command the
best business talent, and the uncertain tenure of
office is also a bar against the acceptance of such
positions. There is no work done by the Mayor
that is so much criticised as his appointments.

Why don't he select men who are well-known engineers, financiers, and business managers? — is a question that is frequently asked, — men who have already made their mark in the community? Few of these men would look at a position in City Hall with the salaries now attached to them. We have had some of the best engineers in the country connected with the building of our Water-Works and Improved Sewerage, but their services have been lost to the city because they were found to be far more valuable elsewhere. Even Mr. Wightman, if he had lived, would not have remained City Engineer for any length of time, because I am aware that he was offered almost double the amount of salary elsewhere.

When our present young City Engineer builds up a reputation his services will also be in demand. Take any one of our departments expending $1,000,000 per year, what business man of large experience will take charge of it for the salary paid? You are forced to take younger men, of untried ability, energy, and integrity; but in many instances these men are objected to by the confirming power because their capacity has not been developed by practical business experience. Honesty and integrity are essential requirements at the head of every department, but business ability is also a necessity. Incompetent men, no matter how honest they may be, will demoralize any department, and are expensive men to the city, even if their services were given gratuitously.

Take, for instance, our Improved Sewerage, one of the greatest works of engineering in this country, and requiring great engineering skill in its management. This work was placed under the Superintendent of Sewers, last year, by a vote of one branch of the City Council, and referred to the next city government at the end of the year by the other branch. The salary of the Superintendent of Sewers is only $3,500 per year, when engineers in almost every city in the country obtain from $6,000 to $10,000 per year.

### THE NEW COURT-HOUSE FOR SUFFOLK COUNTY.

The commissioners appointed by authority of the City Council in February last to make preliminary arrangements for the erection of a new court-house for Suffolk county were in the following month of June vested by the Legislature with the power to take land, with the approval of the Mayor, and to erect thereon a court-house for the use of the courts of the

Commonwealth within and for the county of Suffolk.

Acting under this authority the commissioners, on the 3d day of August, took, in Pemberton square and Somerset street, twenty-one estates, containing 72,502 square feet of land, the assessed value of which was $685,400. To guide them in their settlements with the owners of the property taken the commissioners had a careful appraisal made of the same by five competent experts in the value of real estate.

Of the 72,502 feet of land taken payment has been made for 37,418 feet, the assessed value of which was $324,900, while the appraised value was $368,900, and the amount paid by the commissioner to the owners, $368,740; the owners in all cases giving deeds to the city and paying the taxes assessed for the current financial year.

To meet the expenditures, in part, for this long-needed public building a loan of $850,000, having fifty years to run, was negotiated at three per cent. interest, and one-fiftieth of the principal was made payable annually, instead of accumulating the usual sinking-fund for the payment of the debt at maturity. A further loan of $1,000,000 will be required as the work progresses ; and, by authority of the last

City Council, the Legislature will be asked at its coming session to grant authority to the city to exclude from the operations of the law relating to municipal indebtedness the amount of the Suffolk county court-house loans, as is the case with loans for county buildings in other portions of the State.

The general plans for the new structure are nearly completed, and it is expected that the demolition of the buildings now on the site will commence early in the coming spring.

The plans for the new building do not make provision for the Registry of Deeds or Probate Court.

I am confident that the work done by the Court-House Commission has been excellent, that good progress has been made, and that a new court-house, so long wanted, is now a fixed fact.

### THE DIVISION OF WARDS.

It was the duty of the City Council of 1885 to make the decennial division of the city into new wards. This division becomes necessary because the voting population of the city during each ten years has been extremely migratory. The southern wards have gained largely and the northern wards have diminished. Hence it becomes necessary, as often as once in ten years, to begin with a new apportionment into wards of equal size. Heretofore the city has been allowed to make its own census, but on this occasion the figures were collected by the Bureau of Statistics of Labor. The result was that the census returns were not received by the City Clerk until October, instead of July, as in previous years; but I am not aware that any real harm ensued. The basis of returns rendered, nearly 90,000 legal voters, seems large in view of the registered vote of the city; but it was fixed by law and was beyond our control. It is the same throughout the State, and gives Boston a proper representation proportionately in the House, the Senate, and the Council.

The ordinance passed by the last City Council accordingly divided the city into twenty-four wards, as nearly equal in the number of legal voters as could be arranged. I find not only this rule has been followed, but that the new wards are substantially the old ones, even to the matter of the numbering. As compared with previous divisions there is much less change, and the convenience of the public will be greatly subserved by the conservative action of the Council.

Finding, therefore, that the wards were uniform in population, except Charlestown and East Boston, bounded by wide and prominent streets, and more compact and convenient than those of the previous division, I approved the ordinance. I have regarded it as no part of my duty to consider the political effect of this division. The law does not put that duty upon me, nor is the public interest affected by it. I should have unhesitatingly vetoed any improper division, any attempt to gerrymander the city. But in the present ordinance I see no such improper aim. So long as the wards are equal in population and compact in boundaries I have no right to inquire into the political preferences of the voters. If all of the members of one political party choose to dwell in certain portions of the city I presume that their reasons are satisfactory. So long as every citizen has an uninterrupted opportunity to vote, so long as he is free every year to select his residence, with a view to the exercise of his power as a voter, I hold it to be my duty to regard the ward lines as a part of our municipal system founded solely upon the requirements of law.

I have heard many comments on this division, but I have failed to notice any definite proof of injustice or bad intent. Vague charges should be

entirely put aside, for no man or set of men can
do any injury in a case of this kind unless the
result be immediately apparent.

I may even venture to add that, should the
result of this division be as usual the breaking up
of old political cliques and combinations, the city
will be a gainer. The greatest curse of popular
government is the apathy of the individual voter.
The long continuance of ward lines is apt to lead
to the management of political affairs by local
committees. Ward meetings are cut and dried;
candidates are selected by secret cliques; and the
voter who wishes only the public good becomes
disgusted and ceases to attend to his duties. The
outcry against the present division, as in former
cases, proceeds entirely from the politicians. After
an election in which party lines have been so
largely disregarded, I may be allowed to ask the
public to continue to rely upon their own judgment, and not to discredit the apparently honest
work of last year upon the random assertions of
interested witnesses.

It has even been threatened that an appeal will
be made to the Legislature to set aside the ordinance. As chief magistrate of this great city I
deprecate any such course. Boston has already
suffered in the past from the unwise course of a

minority influential at the State-House. Laws
depend for their efficiency upon the moral belief
in their wisdom and fixity. If every act of the
majority, made in good faith and in conformity
with law, is to be overruled and repealed by the
Legislature, this city sinks below the level of the
smallest village in the State. I do not believe
that Boston has given any cause for such an
appeal, and in the interests of conservatism and
of self-government I trust our citizens will frown
upon all attempts to place us in a position of
tutelage or guardianship. Boston is still able to
manage its own affairs wisely and prudently. The
first step in its downward career will be taken
when the State is requested to interfere in the
management of its local affairs.

### THE PAVING DEPARTMENT.

This department is one of the most important
in the City Government, and one in which there
have been more waste and extravagance than in
any other. I have no hesitation in saying that it
was under bad management during the first six
months of the year 1885, and that it has been
more or less used as a political machine for many
years. The laborers in this department have been
employed to-day and discharged to-morrow, with-

out any system or without any regard for either
the interests of the city or the men employed.
The way the laborers have been used in this department I consider nothing more nor less than
heartless.  This force should be made as permanent as possible.  No man should be discharged
except for cause, and no one should be employed
unless he is capable of doing a fair day's work.

Early in 1885 more than three times the number
of men were on the rolls of the department than
could be employed for any length of time, and
these men were deceived by promises of work that
prevented them from seeking employment elsewhere.  The men for some months past have been
working half-time, rather than cause distress and
suffering by making a radical change.

Since the new charter went into operation the
number of yards has been reduced to ten, and
it is proposed to employ an average of fifty men
at each yard, making a permanent force of five
hundred men.  To this force the department can
give reasonable assurance of permanent employment.  If at times extra work is to be done it
should be understood as such.

A considerable change has also been made in
the number of foremen and sub-foremen.  This
force was largely increased early in the year,

and thousands of dollars have been paid in salaries to men who rendered very little service to the city. The reorganization of the department has not been fully completed. It has taken time to remedy all the abuses that existed, but it is now no longer a political machine, and during the year 1886 will be run on a strictly business basis. The department will also be able to live within the limits of the appropriation, and will not probably require more than $700,000 to do the work during the next financial year.

The amount of money appropriated for this department in April last was $800,000, together with an unexpended balance of $186,917.07 for 1884.

The expenditures have been as follows:—

| | |
|---|---:|
| For Labor . . . . . . . | $475,697 85 |
| Teaming (by contract) . . . . . | 101,281 30 |
| Repairs on Streets, and Miscellaneous Expenses . | 348,080 60 |
| Total expenditures . . . . . . | $925,059 75 |

Of this amount $583,562.08 was expended prior to August 1, leaving a balance on hand December 15 of $61,857.32 to carry on the department till May 1, 1886. This amount is reduced to this figure on account of a large contract for paving-blocks that cannot be used, and is dead material in the hands of the department. We have paid $47,241.33 for paving-blocks, and an additional sum of $69,968.73 is to be paid on contract.

In some previous years the department has done all necessary work with a less sum than the above $61,857.32. In order that the expenditures may be kept within this amount the department must be, and has already been, put upon the most economical basis. Many deserving men of long service have been suspended from labor and the expenditures have been reduced to the minimum. The expense of removing snow, which has varied in the past from $5,000 to upwards of $100,000 in a single season, should always be a matter for special appropriation; as it would be folly to reserve the larger amount for that purpose. While the needs of the department for the coming financial year will not probably exceed that of the present year, and may be reduced to $700,000, a much larger sum would have to be expended if all the demands on the department were met. Our citizens will never be satisfied until our business streets are repaved with more modern style of pavements. The avenues leading to our beautiful suburbs should be kept in good condition, and public expenditures on our streets should ever keep pace with private improvements.

## DEPARTMENT OF PARKS.

The work in this department has steadily progressed during the year, but the present generation scarcely has a practical idea, from their present appearance, how much our parks will add to the beauty of the city, and to the pleasure and sanitary condition of our people some twenty-five or fifty years hence. The cost of the land for the Back-Bay park has been but a small percentage of the cost of construction. The land has been purchased on a thirty-year loan. The construction comes out of the annual tax levy. The cost of the Charles-river embankment will be almost wholly one of construction. I do not see any good reason why this generation should pay the whole expense of an improvement that will be of much greater benefit to future generations. With the West Roxbury, or the Franklin park, as it is now very properly named, it is different. It is already a natural park, and tens of thousands of our citizens, sometimes estimated at 25,000 in a single day, have enjoyed its beauty and pure and bracing air during the summer. In this park no large expenditure is necessary; but some improvement ought to be made every year. The grounds should be cleared, and the avenues and paths commenced on some systematic plan. In Appendix O will be found a brief statement of the work done during the year. The Back-Bay park ought to be completed as soon as possible. Private enterprise is surrounding this park with beautiful and costly dwellings, and the city should encourage the men who are adding so largely to our taxable valuation. The attention of the City Council is called to the closing remarks of the commissioners: —

It would be well to put the parks in condition by a loan rather than by adding the annual expense to the tax levy. The present cost to the citizens would be no more while the citizen of to-day would receive the immediate and full benefit thereof. By this means whatever of benefit and whatever of prosperity is to come from the parks will accrue to our present citizens rather than to those who will flock in to take their places, and the parks themselves put in condition at the least expense.

## MAIN DRAINAGE WORKS.

The Main Drainage Works, or the "Improved System of Sewerage," as they were formerly

called, have been in continuous operation during
the past two years with very satisfactory results.
The sewage of the city having been removed
to Moon Island, and discharged into the outer
harbor, the condition of the bays and docks in
the city is constantly improving.

These works cannot, however, be utilized to
their full capacity in relieving the city of the
sewage nuisances until the radical defects of the
present common sewers be remedied. A complete
survey of these sewers should be made, and,
after a careful study of the subject, plans should
be devised and adopted for the correction of the
existing defects. These defects can never be
ascertained so long as two departments have
charge of our sewerage system, and under any
circumstances the carrying out of these plans
must necessarily be gradual.

The works were designed and built with a view
of ultimately disposing of the sewage from the
high portions of Dorchester, Roxbury, etc., by
means of a high-level intercepting sewer, which
will convey the sewage, without pumping, to
Squantum. For some years to come the low-level
intercepting sewers will receive the sewage from
the low and high level sections of the city, but
it is important that a plan should be definitely

decided upon in order that the common sewers of these districts may be built to conform to the completed Main Drainage System. In this way economic and satisfactory results can be obtained which would otherwise be impossible.

The total amount of appropriation available for the "Improved Sewerage" is $111,922.64, and the amount expended to Dec. 21, 1885, is $5,389,-649.18.

The Main Drainage System should remain under the immediate supervision of the Engineer's Department, as its successful operation depends upon intelligent engineering care, which can be best given by those who have constructed it. In fact, the entire system of sewerage of the city should be controlled by some single department, and as the care, design, and construction of the system is purely a matter of engineering the Engineer's Department is the proper one to be called upon to do the work, and be held responsible for its construction. The office of Superintendent of Sewers need not be abolished, but his work should be done under the direction of the City Engineer. [For further information about our Sewerage System I refer to Appendix M.]

## THE HEALTH OF THE CITY.

It is gratifying to know that the health of the city shows some improvement over previous years. It was generally believed early in the year that our city would be visited by the cholera, and preparations were made to meet this threatened invasion. Some fifty of the leading physicians were called together last January, and, after considering the matter, a committee was selected to advise with the Board of Health as to the best means to meet this emergency. The city was immediately placed in the best sanitary condition possible, and the year has proved to be one of the healthiest on record. The distinguished physicians who were so ready to coöperate with the Board of Health, and whose practical experience and advice were of such great value, deserve the thanks of our citizens generally. The watchful care of the Board of Health has also prevented the spread of small-pox, that has been so disastrous in the neighboring city of Montreal; and I have no hesitation in saying that this Board has done excellent work during the year. The city was never in better sanitary condition than it is to-day, and I am satisfied the Health Commissioners will continue their actual and vigilant work the ensuing year.

There will be almost money enough left from the appropriation to build a new and larger boat to take the place of the one now in use. [For further particulars of the work in this direction see Appendix P.]

### THE PUBLIC SCHOOLS.

The public schools of the city comprise: 1 Normal, 10 Latin and High Schools, 50 Grammar Schools, and 455 Primary School classes. Besides these there are the following special schools, viz., 1 School for Deaf Mutes, 1 for Licensed Minors, 1 Evening High School, 13 Evening Schools, 5 Evening Drawing Schools, and 1 Manual Training School.

The average number of pupils belonging to all these schools during the past year was 59,706, and the number of teachers employed to instruct them 1,418, the cost of maintaining them $1,665,-878.38, while the further sum of $278,114.05 was expended by the City Council for school buildings.

The average cost per pupil during the past year was $27.90, or $1.36 per pupil more than the average cost during the previous year. This increase is in great part accounted for by the decrease in revenue from the sale of books, etc., the amount being in 1883–84 $79,364.66, while

in 1884–85 the amount was only $39,574.76, — a
loss of $39,189.90. This loss was caused by the
legislative enactment which went into effect on
the 1st day of August, 1884, making it obliga-
tory on school committees in towns and cities
throughout the Commonwealth to loan books and
furnish supplies free of charge to the pupils of
the public schools. The next financial year, ending April 30, 1886, will make a better showing.

The past year witnessed the dedication of a
new Grammar School for girls, — the Hyde School,
— a magnificent building, elegant in its structure
and commodious in all its arrangements. The
truant-officers have been rendered much more
efficient than formerly, by a wise and judicious
reorganization of that force. The sanitary condition of the schools has been provided for by
the creation of the office of Professor of Hygiene,
and a new study added by the adoption, as required by law, of a text-book on physiology.

It is with sincere pleasure I bear willing testi-
mony to the zeal and ability with which this
important department of the City Government has
been administered. The high standard which our
schools have attained bears ample proof to the
fidelity with which this great trust confided to
the School Board has been discharged.

MANUAL-TRAINING SCHOOLS.

During the past year manual training has taken more definite form in the work of our schools. There is now a carpenter-shop and two cooking-schools carried on in connection with the schools in the city proper. All the public-school pupils of the city proper can attend these schools. The School Committee propose to recommend the establishment this year of a cooking-school in South Boston and a carpenter-shop in Roxbury. They propose to keep pace with the public demand, and hope in time to be justified in the establishment of a central school for manual training parallel with the Latin and High Schools.

In 1635, five years after the settlement of Boston, the public Latin School was founded, and since then the lawyer, the clergyman, and the like have been conducted up to the doors of the college. In my opinion it will be a great benefit to the community if some of the public money be devoted to manual training. We owe "the worker with his hands" a greater debt than we owe all the professions put together; for "the worker with his hands" makes up over seventy per cent. of the community. Especially is this true when we remember that it is not the hand alone we train, but both hand and mind. Through both the hand and mind we can more easily and naturally build up our boys and girls into broad and good citizens. To my mind no branch of education develops the honesty and character of boys and girls equal to " manual training." Compelled to depend upon themselves to a great extent, — compelled to see that every mistake made is their own, and that any one mistake entails failure, more or less absolute in their work, they receive lessons which always live in their minds. Honest, careful, thorough men and women will be the results.

## THE CITY HOSPITAL.

It would take too much space and occupy too much of your time to notice all the good work done in the City Hospital, one of the greatest of Boston's charitable institutions. The trustees, I am satisfied, have given more attention to the wants of the institution than in any previous year, and a systematic way of conducting the business has been arranged and carried on successfully throughout the year. An examination of the work done and the business methods adopted, it appears to me, would be an advantage to other institutions. The accommodation for out-door patients is altogether inadequate. 47,000 have been attended to during the year, and more room and better facilities are wanted. [See Appendix Q.]

## BOARD OF PUBLIC INSTITUTIONS.

The Board of Directors of Public Institutions have carried on the work economically and with good business ability, but will find it difficult to live within the limit of their appropriation. I regret to say that this is in consequence of the largely increased number of inmates that have had to be provided for. The State institutions are crowded, and insist that we must provide for all our paupers and insane, while, at the same time, every available space in our institutions has been occupied. There is no alternative but to provide for them. I still feel that all our poor and all our criminals ought to be under one management; that our insane asylum should be a branch of the city hospital; and that our truant-children should be separated from the criminals by whom they are now surrounded; but it takes time to bring about reforms, and I regret to say that we have made very little progress since the subject was first agitated. [For a detailed statement of the work done see Appendix J.]

## THE WATER-SUPPLY.

It will be remembered that early in the year
the consumers of water were surprised, on receiving their water-bills, that the rates were advanced without any previous notice. The reason
assigned for this advance was a probable defi-
ciency in the revenue. The advance was so un-
expected and uncalled for, and caused so much
dissatisfaction, that the Water-Board were compelled to reconsider their action, and return to
old rates. It is gratifying to know that this
course has been justified by the facts. The revenue from water has not only been sufficient to
pay all expenses, but will leave a large surplus
in the treasury at the end of the year. With
this favorable condition of the revenue, the Water-
Board have decided to deduct six per cent. from
the water-bills due for year 1886 to all consumers by schedule rate, and later the meter
rates will be revised. This will be gratifying
news to water-takers.

An application has been made to the Legislature for the waters of the Shawsheen, and, if
this application is granted, it is proposed to give
up such parts of the Mystic supply as are liable
to excessive deterioration. I am satisfied that it

is only a question of time when the whole
Mystic supply will have to be abandoned on account of its impurity. [For interesting information
as to the condition of our water-supply see Appendix L.]

### STATE DRAINAGE COMMISSION.

The report to be submitted to the incoming
Legislature by the State Commission appointed in
1884 to consider the subject of the protection
of the public health as endangered by the drainage or by the pollution of the water-supply in
the Charles river, Mystic, Neponset, and Blackstone valleys will be of especial interest to the
citizens of Boston. Among the recommendations
of the commission will be one for the removal
of the dangers which have so long threatened
the purity of the Cochituate and Sudbury river
water-service from the drainage of the towns of
Natick, Framingham, Westboro', and Marlboro', —
all of which have systems of public water-supply
without provisions for sewerage.

The commission will also recommend that the
main intercepting sewer of Boston be continued
from its present terminus on the Back Bay to
Waltham, for the purpose of receiving the sewage
of Brookline, Brighton, Cambridge, Somerville,

Charlestown, Watertown, Newton, and Waltham. This report, affecting as it will so many interests of our city, should be carefully examined by the City Council.

PUBLIC BUILDINGS AND ARCHITECT'S DEPARTMENT.

The work of the department of Public Buildings has been confined to the repairs, alterations, fitting and furnishing, of public buildings and school-houses. The repairs, care, and cleaning of the county buildings are controlled by this department also. The appropriation was $137,354.09 for public buildings and $187,000 for school-houses. The expenditures for the year will come within the amount appropriated. Five new school-houses have been completed the past year, namely: —

Grammar School-house, Hammond street.
Grammar School-house, Minot District.
Primary School-house, Blossom street.
Primary School-house, Harrison avenue.
Primary School-house, Porter street.
Primary School-house, Brighton District.
Primary School-house, Irving Hill avenue.

In regards to the wants of the department for the coming year no extraordinary expenditure beyond the usual amount appropriated will be required except for school-houses, which must be increased on account of the demand made by the Board of Health for new sanitary arrangements in many of the buildings, and the demand of the School Board for improved heating and ventilating apparatus in many of the older houses.

There have also been completed during the year : —

For the Trustees of the City Hospital, a house for nurses on Springfield st.

For the Directors of East Boston Ferries, a new head-house for the South Ferry, and alterations for the North Ferry head-house.

A large hospital building on Deer Island.

A ladder and hose house in Ward 24.

A repair-shop for the Fire Department, on Albany st.

An addition to station-house on East Dedham st., for the Police Department.

There are now in process of erection : —

A Grammar School-house on Dudley st.

A Grammar School-house on Huntington ave.

A Grammar School-house on Winship pl.

A Primary School-house on Medford st.

An Engine-house on Saratoga st.

An Engine-house on Boylston st.

A Police-station on Boylston st.

A house for paupers on Long Island.

A dead-house on Deer Island.

A building for contagious diseases for City Hospital.

These facts indicate that our Architect's department is fully employed.

## THE PUBLIC LIBRARY.

I have placed in an appendix the remarks of the President of the Trustees of the Public Library. Generally speaking, I may say that the Library and its branches have continued to afford the public those facilities for which the public money is granted. It was deemed necessary in 1885 to reduce the annual appropriation by one-twelfth part; and, as the expense of administering the Library is almost a fixed sum, this reduction has been felt mainly in the necessity to stop all intended improvements. Various portions of the city have desired delivery stations or branch libraries, but I cannot advise their establishment until our revenues are more ample.

As to the new building for the Reference Library on Copley square, for which the State and the city have made such generous provision, a delay has occurred which has caused unfavorable comment. I am assured by the trustees that this delay has been caused by a change in plans consequent upon the financial troubles of the past two years. The first plans for a building contemplated the present construction of an edifice large enough to contain the presumed growth of the library for fifty years. The City Architect presented a sketch plan based on these lines, but costing $700,000 or $800,000.

As the appropriation is only $450,000, and there is no reason to think that a larger sum ought to be voted, the trustees decided to reduce their estimates of expense. They believe that at present it would be better to build only enough to provide for the present library with twenty years' increase, so arranging, however, that future buildings can be added as needed without altering the main plan. The City Architect has instructions to design a building to cover the Dartmouth-street front to accommodate all the present library, and to complete the work within the present appropriation. It is expected that this plan will be prepared early next spring.

I must, however, call to your attention the fact that the new charter removes the two official members from the Board of Trustees, heretofore appointed from the City Council. It is a step of doubtful wisdom, although in harmony with the letter of the charter. There is a great difference between having departments managed exclusively by committees of the City Council, and having a minority representation of the City Council placed on permanent Boards. It is a great gain to have a department represented at the City Council by members interested in the subject. This remark applies not only to the Public Library, but to the City Hospital, the Directors of Public Institutions, and the Trustees of Mount Hope Cemetery. All of these are public bodies, expending the public money, and requiring large annual appropriations.

It is clearly proper that these special acts be revised so as to make the number of directors or trustees conform to the fact. It is absurd, for example, to state in one section of an act that there shall be seven trustees of the Public Library, and then allow only five to be appointed.

If, however, the City Council is to be excluded from the management of the Public Library and the City Hospital it may be well to increase these Boards. Nine members, one-third renewable every year, would constitute a Board none too large for the exclusive control of such great enterprises. The larger number and more frequent changes would also give the necessary infusion of new energy and practical ideas. Small Boards holding for long terms are unsuited to our institutions, as they almost invariably degenerate into close corporations. These great Boards require annual appropriations, and their management should truthfully represent the constituencies which provide the means. I suggest, therefore, that some action be taken promptly in the line of one improvement or the other.

### POLICE DEPARTMENT.

A radical change was made in the management of the police force during the past year, by the creation of a Board of Police appointed by the Governor of the Commonwealth.

The new Board entered upon its duties on the 23d of July last. The number of officers and men in the department is 791, and there are now no vacancies. During the year 12 members were discharged, 3 resigned, 5 died, 13 were pensioned, and 28 new members were appointed. Six pensioners died, leaving 79 remaining on the pension-roll.

There were 15 promotions made during the year, viz., one superintendent, one deputy superintendent, one chief inspector, two captains, one inspector, four lieutenants, and five sergeants. All appointments and promotions were made in accordance with the civil-service rules of the Commonwealth.

Capt. Samuel G. Adams, who was superintendent of police from the date of the reorganization of the department in 1878, was retired at his own request, and the vacancy was filled by the promotion of Capt. Cyrus Small, who had served as Deputy Superintendent for the same period.

The station-houses are, with the exception of that in Division 1, in good condition. The remarks made in the last inaugural address relative to Station-house 1 are still applicable, viz.: "The house used by Division 1 is very poorly ventilated, besides being, on account of defects in construction, wholly inadequate to accommodate the large number of prisoners detained therein during the year. The abandonment and sale of this house is recommended, and the erection of a new building, with modern conveniences, off the main thoroughfare; and it is believed that a sufficient sum could be realized from the sale to meet the expenses to be incurred."

The plans for a new station-house on the corner of Boylston and Hereford streets, the erection of which was authorized by the last City Council, were completed, and some progress was made towards erecting the building. It is expected that it will be completed ready for occupancy during the present year.

Measures are being taken to introduce the police signal system into this city. It is the intention of the Board of Police to give the system a practical trial in two or three of the divisions, and then, if it is found to work satisfactorily, to extend it as the necessities of the service require and means will permit. I am happy to say that there has been perfect harmony between the Board of Police appointed by the Governor and the Mayor of the city, and that the work in that department has been satisfactorily performed.

### HORSE-CARS AND STREET-BLOCKADES.

During the entire year 1885 a committee of the Board of Aldermen had under consideration the blockade of our principal business streets by the different horse-railroad companies, but failed to bring about any satisfactory results. Blockades still continue, and horse-cars, partially filled, block our principal streets, to the annoyance of common carriers and citizens generally. I have no hesitation in saying that, as now allowed to run between Cornhill and Boylston street, including Scollay and Dock squares, they have

become a public nuisance. The Board of Aldermen have shown conclusively that they are not
able to cope with this question. Every attempt
on their part has been a failure, and the failure
of the past year has been more pronounced than
in any previous year. I am satisfied that this
blockade of our streets could be easily abated if
the running of horse-cars was placed in the hands
of a permanent commissioner, appointed by the
Mayor, and held responsible to the Mayor, the same
as the heads of the city departments. The principal
nuisance now exists between Cornhill and Boylston street, including Scollay and Dock squares,
and special legislation would have to be obtained
to enable the commissioner to perform his duty.
With such legislation, and a commissioner responsible to the Mayor, horse-car blockades could
be stopped, and the interests of the public better
served.

The Metropolitan, the Highland, the South Boston, the Middlesex, the Union, and the Charles
River horse-railroads now compete with each
other for the passenger traffic of the city. Why
should there be so many competing lines? If these
roads were under one management, if they could
be consolidated with proper regulations and restric-
tions, the public would be better served and the

work more economically performed. Cars partially filled, under such conditions, would not block our principal streets. I have no fear of a horse-railroad monopoly.

The present system is also an expensive one to the city. We are now compelled to employ a large force of police to look after horse-railroads exclusively, who have no other duty, and this force will have to be increased if the present system is allowed to go on. The horse-railroads are a public necessity; but as long as so many companies are allowed to compete with each other they will continue to be, to some extent, a public nuisance unless consolidation is brought about, or until a permanent commission, with special powers, is appointed to regulate them.

### THE LAMP DEPARTMENT.

This department is constantly increasing. Petitions for new lights have been more numerous than in any previous year, and the number that have been placed shows a very large increase. This work has been done without any additional appropriation. The total number of lights added in 1885 was 371. The total in 1884 was 186, showing an increase this year over last year of 185. [See Appendix R.]

## INSPECTION OF MILK.

Excellent work has been done in this department, and its importance is not fully appreciated by our citizens. Since May 1 the department has been reorganized, and the inspection of the important food products with which the office is charged has been rendered. more complete, systematic and effective. Up to the present date there have been 7,600 inspections of milk, 1,500 inspections of butter, and 107 complaints have been made for violations of the statute in relation thereto. The percentage of adulterated samples at the beginning of the year was $38\frac{91}{100}$ per cent. This has been reduced to $14\frac{34}{100}$ per cent., and it is hoped to make it still lower. It is confidently claimed that the quality and purity of the milk supply of the city of Boston have never been better than at the present time.

### REGISTRATION OF VITAL STATISTICS.

The work in this department has progressed in the same accurate and thorough manner that has characterized it in previous years. In regard to the prospective wants of the department, it is desirable that there should be classified indices made to the Births, Marriages, and Deaths for the years 1850 to 1881, inclusive. The number of persons who have occasion to consult the records is so great — and the number is constantly increasing—that it seems to be necessary that the new system of indexing should replace the old. Early last year the Registrar addressed a communication to the City Council recommending this work; but, owing to the illness of the chairman of the committee to whom the communication was referred, the subject failed to receive attention. The suggestion of the Registrar was a good one, and I trust it will receive your attention the coming year.

### BOARD OF REGISTRARS OF VOTERS.

This department is in excellent working condition, and is performing the various duties assigned to it under the laws of the Commonwealth in a manner satisfactory to the citizens. The legislative enactments of the past two years, which apply to . this department, have proved fully adequate to the demands of the public for a thorough and honest registration of the voters; but, if the registration of women is to increase in the proportion that it has this year, additional legislation and increased facilities will soon be required to meet the new conditions occasioned by the change.

## DEPARTMENT OF PRINTING.

This department has furnished all the different documents, memorial volumes, blanks, and stationery required for the use of the City Council and the various departments of the City Government, together with the Record Commissioners' Reports, and the Index to the Minutes of the twelve volumes preceding 1880. These volumes are very important, and have been prepared with great care and at considerable expense, and will prove of value to all who have an interest in the past and present government of the municipality and town.

Owing to the increased demand for copies of the City Documents, by members of the City Council and the public generally, it will be necessary to print a larger edition of each document for the ensuing year, and I would recommend that the edition be increased from 500 copies, the number now printed, to 600 copies.

## RECORD COMMISSIONERS.

The Record Commissioners have completed their tenth year of service, and their published volumes have been, as usual, distributed to our citizens. The large number of regular recipients of these books, including all the colleges, public libraries, and learned societies of the country, is a proof of the economy with which the distribution is made. The warm approval of all students of our history convinces me that the expenditure is a wise one, and worthy of continuance. Other cities and towns are following our example, and Boston has again had the honor of leading in a great public enterprise. The town records have now nearly reached in publication the period of our Revolution, and our citizens will soon have the opportunity of reading the official account of the patriotic and wise course adopted by our predecessors in that momentous struggle with the power of Great Britain. I commend the project to your most favorable consideration.

### THE FIRE DEPARTMENT.

This is one of our most important departments. The property of our citizens depends on active and vigilant work. It is useless to disguise the fact that numerous complaints have been made during the year about the management, but not of sufficient importance to require special action. The material in the department is excellent, but there have not been that harmony and discipline that ought to exist among its members. The attention of the commissioners has been called to these complaints, and there is already a favorable change. The Fire Department might very properly be compared to a military organization, and I believe that if the responsibility were placed under a single-headed commission we would have a more perfect organization. [For details of the work done see Appendix K.]

### NEW CAMBRIDGE BRIDGE.

The new Cambridge bridge failed to receive the approval of the City Council last year, but its necessity and importance cannot be overlooked. Cambridge is closely connected with Boston, and a new avenue is demanded to accommodate and facilitate our trade and business relations with that city. When Cambridge is ready and willing to pay one-half the cost of the structure, it appears to me that Boston should not hesitate. I recommend that a special committee be appointed to take the matter into consideration.

### BRIDGES.

The Albany-street bridge, over the Boston & Albany Railroad, should be rebuilt. The condition of the bridge is such that no repairs are practicable or advisable, and the sidewalks on the bridge have been closed to travel as unsafe. It is believed that the Boston & Albany Railroad Company will pay a part of the cost of rebuilding this bridge.

### THE COMPLAINT-BOOK.

It has been frequently remarked that citizens who have had business with the department, or who have been compelled to make complaints, fail to secure any satisfaction. Since the new charter went into operation a complaint-book has been opened in the Mayor's office, where all complaints are entered. This has been found to work admirably. When the complaint is made in writing, signed by some responsible party, it will be looked into and investigated, and the evil, if any, remedied. I have always found the different departments ready to coöperate with me in this work, and it has very frequently happened that in this way we have received information that is desirable to know. The system will be continued. The officials at City Hall are the agents of our citizens, and when their requests or complaints are reasonable they will secure proper and prompt attention.

## CONCLUSION.

I have referred to various matters that you will be called upon to consider during the year, and trust that the legislative and executive branches of the City Government will work in harmony and for the best interests of the city. We should remember that we represent a city whose credit and standing are second to none in the country, and every member of the City Government should feel that the responsibility rests on him to use his best efforts to keep Boston where she now stands, in the front rank of American cities.

# APPENDIX.

# APPENDIX.

## APPENDIX A.

ASSESSORS' OFFICE, CITY HALL,
BOSTON, December 19, 1885.

HON. HUGH O'BRIEN, *Mayor City of Boston:* —

SIR, — In answer to your request for a statement in relation to the work of the Assessors' Department, I would say, that, omitting all reference to a very large amount of detail in its operations, the principal incidents of the work of the present year may be stated as follows: The valuation of the city, as determined by the assessment of the current year, was $685,579,072. Of this sum $495,973,400 was the estimated value of the real, and $189,605,672 of the personal estate. This is a gain of $2,922,415 over the total valuation of the preceding year. The whole sum ordered to be raised for State, county, and city taxes for 1884 was $11,288,369, and for 1885, $8,693,747; a decrease of $2,594,622. This increase of valuation, and decrease in the amount of money raised, caused the rate of taxation to recede from $17 per $1,000 in 1884, to $12.80 per $1,000 in 1885. The average rate of taxation for the past ten years has been $13.96 on each $1,000. The question of a better method of selecting assessors and assistant-assessors has for many years occupied the attention of the City Council, with but slight change in the ordinance in relation to such elections. But, by the new charter, changes more radical than any ever considered by the government of the city have now the force of law. Under its provisions the assessors are to be appointed by the Mayor, subject to the confirmation of the Board of Aldermen, and their assistants are appointed by the Board of Assessors, subject only to the approval of the Mayor.

The assessment of national bank shares is controlled in a large degree by the laws of the United States. Under the limitations that Congress has imposed the laws of the State require the assessors of the place where any bank is located to assess all its shares. When the assessors of Boston have assessed all the shares of the Boston banks, and after the collector has received the taxes, the treasurer of the city must pay to the Commonwealth the proportion of such taxes that attach to shares belonging to other than citizens of Boston; and the officers of the State credit and pay over the amount received to the several cities and towns where the share-holders reside. The laws of the State, and the methods of the assessors, in taxing this class of property, were subjects of some controversy in former years; but, since the passage of Chapter 315 of the Acts of 1873, all the Boston banks have acquiesced in the law and its administration until the current year. The law, as it now stands, requires the banks to pay the taxes of each of their share-holders. All but six of the Boston banks have this year paid these assessments under protest, and have given notice of an intention to recover the same by suit.

As the judgments, if they prevail, would run against the city of Boston, unless the treasurer retains the money thus collected [amounting to more than $575,000], the city, after it has been compelled to respond to the judgments of the courts, would be powerless to recover this sum which has been assessed and collected by its officers only as agents for others. It would seem that legislation is needed, in order that the city may safely pay over this money, and that those who are interested in defending their right to have, and to retain it, should pay the expense of litigation in the United States courts.

Very respectfully,

For the BOARD OF ASSESSORS,

THOMAS HILLS,

*Chairman.*

## APPENDIX B.

### CITY ARCHITECT'S DEPARTMENT.

This department has had a large number of buildings in process of erection during the past year. The work has been done entirely by contract at exceedingly low figures, and it is the experience of this department that almost all its work is taken by contract at a much lower price than private parties are paying for similar work.

The following buildings have been erected and completed : —

*For the School Department.*

Primary School-house on Harrison ave., Ward 18.

Primary School-house on Blossom st., Ward 9.

Primary School-house in Brighton, Ward 25.

Primary School-house on Parker st., Ward 22.

Primary School-house on Savin Hill ave., Ward 24.

Grammar School-house on Hammond st., Ward 19.

Grammar School-house on Neponset ave., Ward 24.

For the Trustees of the City Hospital, a house for nurses on Springfield st.

For the Directors East Boston Ferries, a new head-house for the South Ferry, and alterations of the North Ferry head-house.

For the Directors Public Institutions, a large hospital building on Deer Island.

### For the Fire Department.

A ladder and hose-house in Ward 24.

A repair-shop on Albany st., Ward 17.

### For the Police Department.

An addition to the station-house on East Dedham st.

### For the Improved Sewerage Department, Park Department, and Water Department.

Several gate-houses.

There are now in the process of erection : —

A Grammar School-house on Dudley st., Ward 20.

A Grammar School-house on Huntington ave., Ward 22.

A Grammar School-house on Winship pl., Ward 25.

A Primary School-house on Medford st., Ward 3.

An Engine-house on Saratoga st., Ward 1.

An Engine-house on Boylston st., Ward 11.

A Police-station on Boylston st., Ward 11.

A House for Paupers on Long Island.

A Dead-house on Deer Island.

A building for contagious diseases at the City Hospital.

For the past two years there has been a marked improvement in the construction of the city buildings in many particulars; elaborate ornament and finish of exterior and interior have been sacrificed for solid and safe fire-proof construction and for the introduction of the most approved appliances for heating and ventilating and sanitary plumbing. As regards the important questions of the ventilation of our public school-houses, the report of the State Board of Health, Lunacy, and Charity, for 1884–85, says: —

" A very important change has been begun within the past year, namely, the introduction of forced ventilation by steam-fans into several houses now building. Credit is due to the present City Architect for this step, which was taken in accordance with the advice of Dr. Billings. An engine of four horse-power, with a fire-pot fourteen inches in diameter, runs two fans, one for propulsion, the other (at the educt shaft) for expulsion. The cost for the plant, for a house of eight rooms, is said to be $2,800 ; the engine can be safely run by an average janitor, and the cost for fuel is trifling. The success of this measure will be a great credit to the city, for all systems dependent on heated flues for the sole motive-power are at times ineffective. In the case of one new school-house, a test of the power exerted in moving one of the fans gave as a result 2.014 horse-power. The calculated power of the machine (disregarding friction in the flues) is such as to enable it to extract all the air from the school-room and the play-grounds in the cellar once in four minutes."

A change in the manner of securing land for public buildings is a matter requiring immediate attention, and an ordinance passed, ordering the City Architect to approve of all lots for public buildings, will obviate the purchase of land that has been found by past experience totally unfit for building purposes.

The plans for the new public library building have progressed as rapidly as the diversified opinions of the trustees would admit. The question of the location of the book-stacks has been settled, and, as the City Council have lately granted the Architect increased facilities for forwarding the work, there is no reason to doubt that the plans will be pushed forward and the work of construction begun in the early spring. The City Architect proposes to associate with him in the work some of the best architectural talent in the country, and to erect a substantial fire-proof library within the limits of the appropriation.

I would call attention to the fact that public buildings constructed under the new ordinance for building lately passed by the State Legislature will require much larger appropriations for their erection than have heretofore been necessary, on account of the increase in thickness of masonry and the large amount of fire-proof material required to be used.

Respectfully submitted,

ARTHUR H. VINAL,

*City Architect.*

# APPENDIX C.

DEPARTMENT FOR THE SURVEY AND INSPECTION OF BUILDINGS,
OLD STATE-HOUSE, December 21, 1885.

HON. HUGH O'BRIEN, *Mayor:* —

DEAR SIR, — In compliance with your request, that I furnish you a brief statement of the work accomplished by this department during the present municipal year, also a statement of the wants of the department, prospectively, for the continuation of its work, I have the honor to submit the following : —

There has been an increased activity in the building interest in all sections of the city, — a decided increase over the previous year.

This has been uniform, and we are constantly adding palatial residences and family hotels, sightly warehouses, large manufacturing establishments, stately mercantile buildings, and imposing public edifices. In addition to these, there has been a very large increase in the number of moderate-cost dwelling-houses erected in our suburban wards, which indicates that the citizens of Boston seeking investments in real property have unlimited confidence in the future of our city.

The tables herewith annexed will show the number of buildings for which permits have been issued during the years 1884, 1885, material of construction, and their ward locations; also the number of completed buildings upon which final reports have been rendered, and their estimated cost (during the year).

The numerous and extensive alterations in our prominent

buildings have required on the part of the department much time, thought, and attention, have involved large expenditures of money, and given employment to a small army of skilled workmen and laborers, and have not only beautified and embellished the property, but have also added large increased valuations to the taxable property of Boston.

By the new Building Laws of our city, which passed the last Legislature and received the signature of His Excellency the Governor on the 19th of June last, together with the Special and Public Statutes and Ordinances of the city, the enforcement of which devolves upon this department, the duties of the department have been largely increased.

The entire work of the department has been performed with untiring energy, and, notwithstanding the great drawbacks, it has been accomplished with comparatively small friction; and I take pleasure in saying that the department has uniformly received the sympathy and hearty coöperation of architects and master-builders in the enforcement of the law.

As to the future wants of the department for the prosecution of its work, I am thoroughly persuaded that the interests of the city will be best served, and more accurate and efficient work rendered by the department, could the area in the districts to which the assistant-inspectors are severally assigned be decreased.

As it now stands they are unable to accomplish the work demanded of them by the statutes and ordinances of the city.

In order to accomplish this work it will be necessary to increase the force of assistant-inspectors by at least two.

The annual report will be submitted early in the year, will contain a complete detail statement of the work accomplished, together with such suggestions in relation to the future construction of our city as experience may demonstrate as essential.

The number of completed brick buildings upon which final reports have been rendered during the year is 350, at an estimated cost of $6,118,400.

The number of completed wooden buildings upon which final reports have been rendered during the year is 1,439, at an estimated cost of $4,478,203.

The number of alterations completed during the year is 1,895, at an estimated cost of $2,367,027.

Thus it will be seen that a capital of $12,963,630 has been invested in the building interests of Boston, as shown by the records of completed work of this department for the year 1885.

The number of permits granted to perform plumbing to December 18 is 2,855.

The number of buildings in which plumbing has been completed to December 8 is 2,370, at an estimated cost of $639,537.

| Wards. | 1885, To Dec. 18th. | | 1884. | |
|---|---|---|---|---|
| | Brick. | Wood. | Brick. | Wood. |
| 1 . . . . . . | . . . . . | 107 | 2 | 26 |
| 2 . . . . . . | 4 | 25 | 1 | 43 |
| 3 . . . . . . | . . . . . | 10 | 1 | 25 |
| 4 . . . . . . | 2 | 36 | 1 | 12 |
| 5 . . . . . . | 3 | 12 | . . . . . | 21 |
| 6 . . . . . . | 14 | . . . . . | 5 | 1 |
| 7 . . . . . . | 4 | . . . . . | 5 | . . . . . |
| 8 . . . . . . | 1 | . . . . . | . . . . . | . . . . . |
| 9 . . . . . | 4 | . . . . . | 4 | . . . . . |
| 10 . . . . . . | 5 | . . . . . | 4 | . . . . . |
| 11 . . . . . . | 106 | 1 | 77 | . . . . . |
| 12 . . . . . . | 23 | . . . . . | 18 | . . . . . |
| 13 . . . . . . | 5 | 28 | 3 | 3 |
| 14 . . . . . . | 8 | 99 | 28 | 71 |
| 15 . . . . . . | 1 | 37 | . . . . . | 46 |
| 16 . . . . . . | 6 | . . . . . | 15 | . . . . . |
| 17 . . . . . . | 4 | 2 | 8 | . . . . . |
| 18 . . . . . . | 8 | . . . . . | 27 | 1 |
| 19 . . . . . . | 19 | 22 | 29 | 21 |
| 20 . . . . . . | 15 | 150 | 11 | 83 |
| 21 . . . . . . | 11 | 118 | 16 | 102 |
| 22 . . . . . . | 76 | 50 | 45 | 76 |
| 23 . . . . . . | 5 | 196 | 4 | 202 |
| 24 . . . . . . | 11 | 301 | 6 | 210 |
| 25 . . . . . . | 2 | 133 | 1 | 129 |
| Total . . . | 337 | 1,327 | 312 | 1,125 |

I am, very respectfully,

Your obedient servant,

JOHN S. DAMRELL,

*Inspector of Buildings.*

# APPENDIX D.

PUBLIC LIBRARY OF THE CITY OF BOSTON,
BOSTON, December 21, 1885.

HON. HUGH O'BRIEN, *Mayor:* —

SIR, — In conformity with the request contained in your favor of the 16th inst. I have the honor to make the following "brief statement" : —

By the new City Ordinance the Trustees of the Library are required to make their annual report in January, instead of the end of the financial year of the city.

The condition of the institution for the first four months of the year was embraced in the totals of the Annual Report made to the City Council. (City Document No. 105.)

Separating the details of the use of books to the first of May, it gives a total of 419,212 volumes. Since that date the issues to the first of December have been 509,391, which, with the estimated deliveries of December, will give a total of 1,030,706 volumes.

The expenditures for the first four months under the old appropriation of $120,000 per annum were $41,179.73. For the last eight months, under the reduced appropriation, there has been withdrawn from the city treasury $69,987.45, which is within the monthly average that the Trustees were authorized to expend. The reduction has mainly fallen upon the purchases for popular reading.

On the first of May there were in the Bates Hall Library, inclusive of bound newspapers and duplicates, 289,917 volumes, and in the popular libraries 164,030 volumes. The total increase since has been 8,265 volumes, making the whole number of books in the whole collection 462,212.

The salaries paid for the library service are uniformly moderate, and in many instances too low. The city has every reason to be satisfied with the quality of the work done.

By the general terms of the donations to the library of the trust-funds their interest is expended in books of permanent value, which are added to the Bates Hall collection.

Negotiations are in progress for a rearrangement of the contract with the Trustees of the Fellowes Athenæum, at Roxbury, by which it is expected that the expenditures for the Roxbury branch will be reduced.

It is to be hoped for the usefulness of the institution that the appropriation for expenditures of $10,000 per month, or $120,000 per annum, will be restored from first of May. Its popularity with the larger number of readers in the city and districts depends mainly upon its ability to purchase the current books of interest of the day.

## LIBRARY BUILDING.

By the order of the City Council, approved by the Mayor on the 31st March of the present year, "the City Architect is directed to prepare plans for a library building to be erected on the lot of land on Dartmouth street held by the city for that purpose, and to submit the same to the Trustees of the Public Library for their approval."

The problems of the construction of this most important edifice appear to be in a fair way of solution, the larger difficulty having apparently been overcome. It is hoped and expected that work will be begun in the early spring, and that a fire-proof building, well ventilated and warmed, and well lighted throughout, with sufficient storage for books, and with such convenience of access and use as will meet its large requirements, will be constructed without exceeding the amount of the proposed loan for this object.

Respectfully yours,

W. W. GREENOUGH,
*President Trustees Public Library.*

## APPENDIX E.

Office of the Clerk of Committees, City of Boston,
City Hall, December 19, 1885.

*To His Honor Mayor* Hugh O'Brien : —

Dear Sir, — In response to your request for a statement regarding the work of this office the past year, etc., I have to say that the work itself is mainly of a clerical nature, and involves attendance upon the various committees of the City Council, the keeping of records for them, and the preparation of their reports and papers to be presented to the City Council. In addition to these, that might be termed regular duties, the clerk is expected to furnish information and service of varied character to individual members of the City Council, city officials, and to a certain extent to the public at large.

We have had charge of 94 committees this year, which may be classified as follows : Standing, 32 ; special, 31 ; nominating, 31. Number of committee meetings attended by the clerk and his assistants to the present time, 521.

Among the more important matters that have been considered by the committees may be mentioned the Revised Ordinances, as prepared by the commission appointed to make the changes that were required under the "new charter" (Chap. 266, Acts of 1885) ; the investigation of the action of the Water Board regarding the purchase of land on Fisher Hill as a reservoir site for the high-service system, one of the most protracted and extensive investigations ever conducted in City Hall; the investigation of the contract of the Water Board for purchasing pumping-machinery of the Worthingtons, of New York; the horse-car blockades; the memorial services in honor of Gen. U. S. Grant, arranged by a special committee; the decennial division of the city into wards.

The consolidated index to the City Council proceedings, prepared by Mr. W. H. Lee, the former clerk, has been completed and published this year.

The work of superintending licensed minors, receiving their applications, etc., formerly carried on by the truant-officers, has been placed upon this department on account of the School Committee relinquishing it the past summer.

The "new charter" has in a great measure abolished -the powers formerly exercised by committees, and their labors have been proportionately reduced, but the business of the office has not been lessened in consequence, although its character has been changed somewhat on account of the new law.

I should not consider our present force more than will be necessary to enable us to properly perform the labor required of us.

Very respectfully yours,

JAMES L. HILLARD,
*Clerk of Committees.*

# APPENDIX F.

SEALER'S OFFICE, December 21, 1885.

*To His Honor the Mayor:* —

In accordance with your request, I hereby hand you a statement of the doings of this department from January 1, 1885, to date: —

| | | |
|---|---|---:|
| Number of Scales tested | . . . . | 8,314 |
| " Weights " | . . . . | 32,364 |
| " Dry measures, tested | . | 5,209 |
| " Wet " " | . | 6,606 |
| " Yardsticks " | . . | 496 |
| " Charcoal baskets " | . . | 6 |
| " Coal " " | . . | 93 |
| " Grain tubs " | . | 4 |

| | | |
|---|---|---:|
| Amount received for sealing | . . . | $2,918 86 |
| " " adjusting | . . . . | 164 01 |
| Total amount received . | . . . . | $3,082 87 |

Previous to May 1, 1881, all portable scales, weights, and measures were brought to the Sealer's office, for sealing and adjusting, free of expense. This system was unsatisfactory to merchants of the city, inasmuch as all their scales could not be spared from their places of business at the same time, and several trips to the Sealer's office were thereby necessitated. With a view to remedying this inconvenience the Committee on Markets, Weights, and Measures changed the system so that those that preferred sealing at their places of business could be accommodated by payment of the fees provided in the Public Statutes.

Now the merchants that aim at keeping their scales, weights, and measures correct, complain much at the payment of *any* fees for inspecting and sealing, especially when they are found by the Sealer to accord with the standards. They claim that the purchasing public are protected by sealing against *incorrect* or *false* weights, while they must pay, notwithstanding their scales, weights, and measures are found to be correct.

I would respectfully recommend for Your Honor's consideration that all fees be abolished, and that all testing, adjusting, and sealing be done free of expense to owner of same.

Respectfully submitted,

MICHAEL D. COLLINS,
*Sealer of Weights and Measures.*

## APPENDIX G.

DECEMBER 18, 1885.

HON. HUGH O'BRIEN, *Mayor:* —

DEAR SIR, — Mount Hope Cemetery contains one hundred and six and three-fourths ($106\frac{3}{4}$) acres of land, one-half being converted into lots, graves, avenues, walks, and borders, seven (7) miles of which are avenues and walks, and fourteen (14) miles borders. The avenues and walks are to be kept clean and in repair, and the borders are lawn-mowed once a week through the season. We have raised and planted one hundred and fifteen (115) thousand plants, and cared for the same. We have six hundred and seventy-five (675) lots to care for, one hundred and seventy-five (175) of which are under perpetual care. Nearly two acres of filling have been completed from four (4) to eight (8) feet deep. This, with the usual number of graves to be prepared for the public lot and city poor, with the partial completion of fifty-two (52) lots, constitutes the most part of work performed thus far. There are a number of incidentals, such as foundations for head-stones and monuments and repairing of various kinds. That part of the cemetery known as the city poor lot is nearly consumed for the burial of the city poor, and it would be advisable for the city to look ahead to its future needs. The time will come, and at no distant day, when we must have more land for our city poor, and the longer the delay the greater the price. There is land that we can get at a fair price to-day; what the price will be a year from now none can tell. I hope I have given you the desired information; if not, I shall be pleased to enlighten you further in the matter, if I can.

Respectfully yours,

J. E. E. GOWARD,
*Superintendent.*

# APPENDIX H.

OFFICE OF SUPERINTENDENT OF HEALTH,
BOSTON, December 22, 1885.

HON. HUGH O'BRIEN, *Mayor:* —

DEAR SIR, — In reply to your circular of December 16, requesting a statement of the work done by the Health Department the past year, I have to report that the work of collecting ashes and garbage, cleaning streets and cesspools in the city proper has been performed in a satisfactory manner; but few complaints have been received. In the outlying district the work has not been satisfactory. The ashes and garbage should be removed with more regularity. To do this work additional teams and men will be required for the coming year.

The estimates of expenditures of the Inspector of Milk have always been placed with those of this department. They have been small until the last two years, not over five hundred dollars above the salaries. Now they call for several thousands. I believe they should conduct their department independent of ours.

This department has employed three teams for conveying prisoners from the several station-houses to the court-house, jail, and boat. These teams should be under the charge of the Police Department, and I would suggest they be transferred to said department, the expense to be charged to them.

An additional appropriation of $12,000 will be required at

once to pay for the Barney Dumping Boat, for which no estimates were made in this year's appropriation.

Respectfully submitted,

GEO. W. FORRISTALL,

*Superintendent.*

## APPENDIX I.

OFFICE OF THE

BOARD OF DIRECTORS OF EAST BOSTON FERRIES,

EAST BOSTON, December 19, 1885.

HON. HUGH O'BRIEN, *Mayor:* —

DEAR SIR, — I have the honor to acknowledge the receipt of your communication, and in reply would respectfully state that the expenditures and receipts for this department in the year 1885, including drafts and requisitions, drawn this month to date, have been as follows : —

EXPENDITURES.

| | | |
|---|---|---:|
| On account of new tank . . . | | $147 50 |
| "  new slips . . . . | | 12,220 80 |
| "  new head-house . . . | | 30,880 95 |
| "  current expenses and repairs . | | 225,946 32 |
| | | $269,195 57 |

RECEIPTS.

| | |
|---|---:|
| From tolls, etc., from January 1, 1885, to December 19, 1885 . . . . . | $151,327 06 |
| Estimated from December 19, 1885, to January 1, 1886 . . . . . . . | 5,330 00 |
| Rent due and payable January 1, 1886 . | 631 67 |
| | $157,288 73 |

The boats are in a very good condition, except the steamer "Lincoln," and I would respectfully renew the request made by the Board, in the annual estimate of 1885–6, for a new boat to take her place. The drops and slips are also in good condition, except the slips on East Boston side of the South Ferry, which will need some repairs.

The buildings on Boston side of both ferries are in first-class condition, having been built within three years, but those on East Boston side should be replaced with new ones to correspond, as they are far from being what is required.

I would state that the average daily travel is about 25,000 foot-passengers and 1,800 teams.

I would further state that during the year a change has been made in the method of selling and the collection of tickets, and when the public become accustomed to the change, and the system perfected, I think there will be no cause for complaint.

I have the honor to be
Your obedient servant,
E. PEARL,
President.

## APPENDIX J.

OFFICE OF THE
BOARD OF DIRECTORS FOR PUBLIC INSTITUTIONS,
BOSTON, December 21, 1885.

HON. HUGH O'BRIEN, *Mayor of Boston:* —

DEAR SIR, — The Board of Directors, in reply to your request, submit the following : —

A question of vital importance, as it affects the government of the institutions, is the question : Of how many members the Board shall consist. By the original act of incorporation, the first section of Chapter 35 of the Acts of 1857, it is provided that the Board shall consist of twelve resident citizens of the city, and Section 4 of the same act prescribes the manner in which they shall be chosen, viz. : nine citizens at large, one member of the Board of Aldermen, and two members of the Common Council.

By the provisions of the new city charter any representation of the City Council on any Board is directly prohibited. This act of course vitiates, in part, Section 4 of the act of incorporation of our Board, and still does not repeal the first section, which declares the Board shall consist of twelve, except by inference.

This uncertainty can only be removed by appropriate legislation, which we would respectfully suggest you should recommend.

During the year just closing the capacity of the institutions has been severely taxed. At the present time beds have been placed in the corridors of two of the pauper institutions, and Deer Island has never been crowded as it now is ; while the Lunatic Hospital, at South Boston, is so very much overcrowded as to be of no practical benefit for hospital purposes, thus making it almost impossible to effect a cure.

With every inch of available space taken up, the inability of the institutions to furnish proper accommodations for Boston's charges becomes every day more apparent, and the advisability of pushing forward with all possible speed the erections of buildings on Long Island to accommodate all Boston's paupers, male and female, cannot be questioned.

The removal of the female paupers from Austin Farm to Long Island, when the proposed building is completed, will relieve, in some measure, the Lunatic Hospital by the removal of the chronic cases.

A very important matter is the question of appropriations. For · years the Board has been reducing its expenses as well as could be done with the ever-increasing number committed to their charge, and this year they asked for a much less sum than was asked the year before. The amount was exactly what it cost to run the institutions for the year previous; but when it was submitted to the Government it was cut down indiscriminately, far below a living figure. Then came the Limitation Act of the last Legislature, and a horizontal reduction of ten per cent. was again made, though the reduction might better have been made in other directions. The result is there is not money enough to pay the expenses for the year. Our appropriations have suffered in like manner before, and as our expenses are in all cases entailed on us by the Court, they of course must be met; and, as the result of the present system, we are obliged to make repeated demands on the Government. It does appear to us that some other method of making appropriations for what are practically fixed charges should be recommended.

Boston sets the example for most of the institutions of the country; but while her system is excellent, her humanity unsurpassed, and her care of the needs and comfort of her unfortunates unequalled, yet her buildings are far below the standard of many of our sister cities. And we feel that when this want is met Boston's poor and unfortunate will be better taken care of for less money than in any other city in the Union.

Yours very respectfully,

J. H. O'NEIL,

*President Board of Directors.*

# APPENDIX

Office of the Board of Fire Commissioners,
City Hall, Boston, December 21, 1885.

*To His Honor* Hugh O'Brien, *Mayor, City of Boston:* —

Sir, — In reply to your request of the 16th inst., the Board of Fire Commissioners herewith submits a brief statement of facts concerning this department the past year.

The organization of the department during the year has not materially changed. It consists of, besides the Board of Commissioners, the Chief Engineer and Assistants, 32 Engine Companies, including the Fire-boat Co., 14 Ladder Cos., 10 Independent Hose Cos., 6 Chemical Engine Cos., a Water Tower, and Aerial Ladder Co., a force of 336 permanent and 309 call-men.

By the resignation of Engineer Cunningham, of District 3, Engineer Abbott, of District 6, was transferred to that district, and under the civil-service rules Capt. John A. Mullen, of Engine Co. 15, was promoted to fill the vacancy.

The houses of the department are in good condition, and have received from time to time the necessary attention to keep them in comfortable and good order. During the year the new house, for the accommodation of Ladder Co. 9, and Hose Co. 1, on Main street, Charlestown, has been completed and occupied. The new house on Saratoga street, East Boston, is fast approaching completion, and is expected to be ready for occupancy by March next.

The foundation for the new house to be erected on the corner of Boylston and Hereford streets is being laid.

A lot of land has recently been purchased for an engine-house on Monument street, Charlestown, and it is proposed to locate Hose Co. 4 there when completed.

The Apparatus Repair-Shop, located at the corner of Albany and Bristol streets, has been completed, and thoroughly fitted with new machinery of improved pattern ; the building is also used as a storehouse for supplies and spare apparatus.

The apparatus is in general good condition. Contracts have been made for building a new chemical engine to be located in East Boston, also for a new ladder truck.

The hose, about 70,000 feet in all, is in serviceable condition. Contracts for some 6,000 feet have been recently made.

The horses, some 166 in number, are in good condition. No serious epidemic has appeared during the year. Old age or other troubles necessitates a renewal of about 12 per cent. of the horses annually.

The city has been remarkably free from extensive fires.

The total number of alarms was 778, and the loss on buildings and contents about $1,200,000. The number of fires whose loss exceeded $20,000 was 11.

The Fire Alarm Telegraph branch of the department is under the charge of a superintendent, who is assisted by the following subordinates : one assistant-superintendent, three operators, one foreman of construction, ten linemen, and one battery-man.

Some new apparatus has been added and other improvements made at head-quarters, and reconstruction of the circuits completed at the South End, North End, and Roxbury, with several new gong circuits, and extended telephones requiring the use of 84 miles of new wire, with the necessary equipment of insulators, etc., and 133 poles. There are about

350 miles of wire, making 49 bell-strikers, 96 gongs, 42 tappers, and 59 telephones.

Respectfully submitted,

H. W. LONGLEY,

*Chairman Board of Fire Commissioners.*

---

# APPENDIX L.

---

BOSTON WATER BOARD OFFICE,

December 21, 1885.

HON. HUGH O'BRIEN, *Mayor:* —

In response to your circular of the 17th inst., the Boston Water Board present the subjoined summary of the condition of their department.

Of the works of construction, which were in progress at the date of the last report of the Water Board to the City Council, the Dam and Basin No. 4 are completed within the estimates.

The conduit across Farm Pond should have been completed, according to the contract, October 1, 1885, but, although an extension of two months was granted to the contractors, they failed to complete the work. It is, however, so far advanced that it can be finished, ready for use, by June 1.

The high-service works, for which the City Council of 1884 appropriated $765,000, and for which the principal reservoir site has been located at Fisher Hill, may be so far completed by the end of 1886 as to put into use the reservoir at the point named, provided there be no hindrance as to the construction of reservoir and pumps. You are aware that there is an unsettled question as to the pumps, upon which the action of the City Council is required.

The condition of the reservoirs and supply is such that the contemplated cleansing of Basin 3 can be safely and advantageously done during the coming season.

The existing appropriations for additional supply will undoubtedly meet the cost of this work.

It is not expected that any new works of construction or repair requiring any considerable expenditure of money will be undertaken during 1886, unless they arise from legislation respecting new sources of supply, or as a sequence of the drainage projects, which are also to be the subjects of legislative consideration.

As estimated at the beginning of the financial year there will be a considerable surplus of revenue in the Cochituate . department, if the prescribed water-rates are maintained.

The supply is at present ample, and promises to be so during the coming year. The consumption *per capita* has fallen off gradually to an average of less than 70 gallons per head per day. This is due to several causes, among which are the use of waste detectors, the surveillance of inspectors, the discrimination of rates against wasteful fixtures, and, to a very limited extent, the application of meters.

The Meter Division has for some time labored under the disadvantage of operating with a large number of faulty meters, and some months may elapse before we can place matters in this. division on a satisfactory footing. In that division, and also in that of inspection and waste, the expenses have been unnecessarily large. We have made some reductions of force.

The quality of the water has been considerably improved, and it is to-day fully equal to that of any large city in America. But the possibilities of improvement are not exhausted, and we shall continue our efforts in this direction. As the City Council has authorized an application to the Legislature for the waters of the Shawshine, they are substantially advised that it is hoped to substitute these waters for such parts of the Mystic supply as are liable to excessive deterioration. If a legislative grant shall be obtained the matter of methods to be adopted in making available the new supply will be the subject of timely communication. By authority of the City Council special surveys in the line of this inquiry have been authorized, and under our direction they have already been begun by the City Engineer.

Boston Water Board, by

H. T. ROCKWELL,

*Chairman.*

## APPENDIX M.

Sewer Department, City Hall,

Boston, December 20, 1885.

Hon. Hugh O'Brien : —

Dear Sir, — In answer to your request for a statement in relation to work done by the Sewer Department during the past year, I would say that the department has built about 12½ miles of sewers, and expended $319,864.98.

A main sewer has been built in Washington street, from Forest-Hills station to Roslindale, to drain a district which has needed a system of sewerage for a number of years. Also a main sewer in Dorchester District across the low land lying between Washington street and Blue-Hill avenue, which has opened for building purposes some five hundred acres of land, upon which considerable building has been done during the past year.

Also two large main sewers have been built in the Brighton District, which will drain a district heretofore undeveloped.

There are at the present time a considerable number of sewers draining into that portion of Stony Brook between Huntington avenue and Beacon street, which should at once be removed.

There has been an unusual number of small sewers built during the year. The demand for these sewers in districts not covered by a loan has been so great and the appropriation so small that the committee have not felt warranted in taking any action on a number of petitions now on file in this office.

There have been about 155 catch-basins built during the year to take the surface water from the streets, and the amount needed yearly for this kind of work should not be stinted if we wish to have our streets kept in good condition.

The department is now at work on an intercepting sewer between Crescent avenue and Greenwich street, in the Dorchester District, to take the drainage now emptying into Dorchester Bay. This will not be in operation until next summer.

It will be necessary the coming year to drain the district about Ashmont station, and to accomplish this a main sewer should be built from Neponset avenue to Ashmont station.

As the care and maintenance of Stony Brook are in charge of this department there will have to be a separate appropriation, or an amount included in the regular one, to keep the walls in repair; and as a greater part of the brook is an open channel, it becomes necessary to clean the same about twice a year.

This department has, in accordance with your recommendation, made a survey of all the old sewers in the city proper, East and South Boston, and Charlestown districts, and, with the aid of a generous appropriation, will put the sewers in those districts in a suitable condition. Some of these will have to be rebuilt; but the greater part of them can be repaired at a moderate cost, so as to be made serviceable for a number of years to come, and are not so defective as some people imagine.

This department has constructed and under its control about 238 miles of sewers, while the Engineer's Department controls the main outlet, about $13\frac{1}{2}$ miles. While the duty of providing for the successful drainage of the whole city falls directly upon the Sewer Department, and it is held responsible for all shortcomings, the ultimate disposal of sewage is beyond its control.

The Board of Aldermen passed an order giving this department control of the whole, and the Common Council voted to refer the subject to the next City Government. I can only add that, in my judgment, this department should have entire control of the whole system.

Very truly yours,

THOMAS J. YOUNG,
*Superintendent of Sewers.*

# APPENDIX  N.

———

Office of the Board of Street Commissioners,
City Hall, Boston, December 22, 1885.

Hon. Hugh O'Brien, *Mayor:* —

Sir, — Replying to your request of the 16th inst., the Board of Street Commissioners submit the following statement of their work during the municipal year now ending : —

In the city proper streets have been widened by taking 9,388 square feet of land, the estimated damages therefor being $3,865. 548 feet in length of private ways have been built out as public streets of the city.

In Roxbury, widenings, extensions, and alterations have been made to the extent of 6,896 square feet of land taken, the estimates being $10,522.25. 1,643 feet in length of private streets have been made public.

Dorchester : street widenings have taken 53,883 square feet, estimated $2,200. 7,755 feet of private ways have been accepted as public streets.

West Roxbury has had widenings made of 1,071 square feet, estimated to cost $1,121. 4,278 feet of private ways have been made public.

Brighton has had private ways, of a total of 1,695 feet in length, accepted as public streets.

East Boston : 2,282 square feet taken for street alterations, estimated damages being $4,307. 2,450 feet of private streets accepted.

In South Boston 1,326 feet of private streets made public.

Discontinuances have been made of 37,190 square feet of old Warren Bridge, at Charlestown, and of the streets at South Boston Point east of Q street, and in the park land, aggregating 5,830 feet in length.

An addition of the foregoing shows a total of 72,449 square feet, or about $1\frac{2}{3}$ acres, taken for street improvements in the whole city during the year, the estimated damages therefor being $20,894.25, and 19,695 feet, or about $3\frac{2}{3}$ miles of private streets made public, with 5,830 feet, or about $1\frac{1}{10}$ miles of public streets discontinued.

A large part of the laying out of new streets during the year has been to meet the immediate calls for water-supply and drainage.

The Commissioners are not aware of any projected street improvements for the ensuing year that will require a large expenditure of money, and the usual appropriation for the ordinary work of laying out and widening streets is probably all that will be called for in the annual estimates.

Very respectfully,

ISAAC H. WRIGHT,

*Chairman Board of Street Commissioners.*

# APPENDIX O.

DEPARTMENT OF PARKS, CITY OF BOSTON,
December 23, 1885.

*To His Honor Mayor* O'BRIEN : —

DEAR SIR, — This Board has received your communication inquiring what has been accomplished by this department up to the present time, and its prospective wants.

The Back Bay Improvement has progressed, fulfilling the expectations of the Commissioners and the Engineers. Situated in marsh lands and flats, the place was formerly a great nuisance by being also the receptacle of the drainage of a considerable population. It is rapidly assuming a somewhat comely appearance. The nuisance formerly existing there has been entirely removed, and by means of ample and skilfully constructed conduits the waters of Stony Brook and Muddy River are under control; the waters of the basin can be changed at will, and the bay kept in a condition to add to instead of militating against the health of the city.

The Commissioners desire, if the means can be afforded them, to complete during the coming year the lower basin approached from Beacon street, Commonwealth and Westland avenues, and to build the bridge opposite the Westland avenue entrance to Audubon road. This will add to the value of the lands in the vicinity on the city side and bring into use lands beyond.

The purchase of lands for the Muddy River Improvement goes on, but slowly. This has not proved a loss to the system of parks, as all the money the City Government has been disposed to allow for construction has found outlets in other directions.

Not much money has been expended in Franklin park, formerly West Roxbury park. Still, in the summer it is visited daily by thousands of our overtaxed people in search of rest and recreation. Though the Commissioners have felt much gratification at the benefit to the public of this park in its present comparatively wild condition, they still are desirous that some of its features may from time to time show themselves. They would accordingly like to clear the grounds of that part which has been called the Playsted, complete the overlooking terrace, and the roads around the Playsted.

Bussey park and Arnold arboretum, by the joint labors of the city and Harvard College, give evidences of the beautiful spot it is destined to be. The city has already expended $60,000 of the $75,000 it is required to expend upon the roads of this park by its contract with Harvard College. There is no provision for any completion of these roads except by the city. The expenditure of a larger than the contract sum is necessary, and no expenditure can be put to a better use than to complete these roads, where all else will be done by others to make it one of the most interesting places in the country.

At the Marine park, City Point, the Commissioners are constructing, of wood, what they have called a temporary pier, because it is intended in the end to be supplanted by solid filling. It is also intended to construct an iron pier beyond the temporary one. This is so important a feature of this park that the Commissioners think nearly everything else can await its completion.

Neptune road, leading to Wood Island park, has been graded and loamed for trees. The desire of the Commissioners is to build the bridge over the railroad, thereby connecting Neptune road with the park itself.

The Charles-river Embankment will require an expenditure for roads, paths, planting, etc., after it has been graded.

If permitted, the Commissioners would suggest that it would be well to put the parks in condition by a loan rather than by adding the annual expense to the tax levy. The present cost to the citizens would be no more, while the citizens of to-day would receive the immediate and full benefit thereof.

By this means, whatever of benefit and whatever of prosperity are to come from the parks will accrue to our present citizens, rather than to those who will flock in to take their places, and the parks themselves be put in condition at the least expense.

For the Board,

BENJAMIN DEAN,

*Chairman.*

---

## APPENDIX P.

---

### BOARD OF HEALTH.

Hon. Hugh O'Brien, *Mayor of Boston:* —

Dear Sir, — At your request we herewith transmit a brief statement of the work of the department for the past year and the sanitary condition of the city at the present time. In anticipation of a possible visitation of cholera to this country the spring cleaning of the streets, courts, alley-ways, yards, and vacant lots, and the removal of all winter collections of filth and rubbish in and about dwellings, were begun earlier than usual and have been vigorously prosecuted throughout the season.

A large number of ponds of stagnant water have been drained off and spaces left covered with gravel.

Many thousands of feet of drain have been built by the Board where neither the Sewer Department could do the work nor the individual owners be made to agree to do it themselves.

Many wells have been found in the built-up parts of the city, the waters examined, and, wherever found unfit for domestic purposes, the wells have been condemned and filled up.

At the instance of the Board of Health last winter the Legislature passed an act authorizing the Board to cause the abolishment of all privy-vaults where there are sewers in the streets adjoining; and under this law the Board has already caused to disappear hundreds of the worst nuisances that our city has ever had to contend with.

The Board will renew its work of destroying privy-vaults early in the spring.

The work of removing foul and waste materials beyond the limits of the city is now well provided for by the recent purchase of a patent scow, which is especially adapted for this work.

School-houses, tenement-houses, and other places occupied by large numbers of persons have been systematically visited, and wherever faults have been found they have been corrected as far as the Board has found it practicable to do.

Quarantine has been administered with uninterrupted vigilance, and no case of cholera, yellow fever, or any other exotic disease has found entrance into our city during the season.

A large amount of additional work has been done in quarantine, owing to the examination of all vessels from Canada and the Provinces, and there has been a corresponding increase in the income for that department.

The general health of the city during the past year has been good, and for the last six months exceptionally so.

The mortality from preventable diseases has been almost unprecedentedly low, and compares most favorably with that of other large cities in this and foreign countries.

Contagious diseases, the bane of all large cities, have been dealt with to the full extent of the means given to the Board of Health.

Small-pox prevailed in this city almost continuously from 1840 to 1873, when, in the midst of a great epidemic of this disease, the Board of Health was given full power and facilities for suppressing the epidemic. The almost complete absence of small-pox from our city during the following twelve years, the feeling of security against this pestilence by our people, and its effect upon the business interests of the city are too well known to need further comment here.

The Board of Health complains that, while ample provision is made for the care of small-pox patients, almost no means are afforded for the isolation of scarlet fever and diphtheria, and that the Board is almost helpless in its desire to prevent the spread of these two diseases. The number of deaths from scarlet fever and diphtheria in Boston last year was 515, and the average for the last five years is 695.

The Board thinks that this mortality from two contagious and preventable diseases is not creditable to our city, and need not occur if sufficient hospital accommodations are furnished in which to isolate the patients.

The Board has repeatedly asked for the hospital accommodations; but as yet the means for isolating those diseases have not been supplied.

There is reason to believe that the thorough sanitary work performed during the year has been a large factor in reducing the mortality.

The Board of Health will not only keep its expenses within its appropriation, but hopes to provide from it a portion of the cost of the new steamer for quarantine.

Respectfully submitted,

For the BOARD OF HEALTH,

S. H. DURGIN,
*Chairman.*

# APPENDIX Q.

CITY HOSPITAL, BOSTON,
December 22, 1885.

HON. HUGH O'BRIEN, *Mayor of Boston :* —

SIR, — In the absence of the president of the trustees, Hon. T. J. Dacey, I give on his request a brief statement of the facts of the work done in this department during the hospital year, May 1, 1885, to date.

The amount of the annual appropriation for this fiscal year was $165,000. There was a balance of trust funds not used last year of $1,810.55, which gave us a total credit for the year of $166,810.55. The expenditures so far during this year, including the draft of January 1, 1886, will amount to $121,370.72. This expenditure is well within the limits of allowance for the nine months now past, and will show a *pro rata* surplus for that period of $3,737.19. I estimate that the balance for the remaining three months will be adequate to meet the expenditures for that period. I do not anticipate, however, that there will be any surplus at the end of the fiscal year. The average number of patients during these three coming months is always the largest of the year; our expenditures for subsistence, fuel, light, and other supplies are also larger. These demands upon us will undoubtedly consume the accrued surplus; but I feel warranted in saying that this department will not call for any further appropriation for maintaining the hospital during the rest of the fiscal year.

In regard to the amount of work done, in the care and treatment of the sick, this year has proved no exception to the last three or four years in this respect, that the hospital each year has a larger average number of patients treated than each previous year. The number for the year 1883-4 averaged sixteen more daily than 1882-3; the year 1884-5 was twenty more than in 1883-4; our daily average for the nine months of this year has been twenty-one more than last year, or forty-one more than two years ago.

The class of cases treated is each year more closely restricted to the more acute and severe cases, the movement of the ward population is more rapid, and the hospital serves more closely its real purpose in giving its benefits to the greatest number of people.

The event of the hospital year has been the completion and occupation of the new dormitory for nurses. The building now accommodates 69 nurses, and has been in use long enough to prove its utility, and to demonstrate the desirability in placing the nursing force in apartments outside the wards. The health of the nurses has been improved, and the hospital is benefited by receiving not only more constant but a better quality of labor.

The rooms vacated by nurses are nearly all devoted to the use of patients. Our accommodations have been increased by 48 beds; not only can we accommodate this increased number, but we can do our work better and more humanely. It particularly enables us to place in isolating rooms patients who are dangerously ill, delirious, or dying, who formerly were treated in the open wards. Our accommodations for contagious diseases are likewise increased by 20 beds, and so far this year we have rejected no applicant with contagious disease for want of room.

Much work has been done during this year in the way of

renovating and general repairs. The amount of wear and tear in a building occupied by five and six hundred people of the class we receive here is always very great. A more frequent renovating is required here than in ordinary public buildings, because our wards and rooms are sooner polluted, and the very object of the hospital is the restoration to health. Again, we cannot safely treat the sick except by classification and separation. This involves a large number of buildings, which are more expensive to maintain and repair than if the patients were aggregated in one structure.

Several of the wards have been vacated in turn, and thoroughly cleansed and renovated.

As a whole our buildings are probably in a better condition of repair than at any time in the history of the hospital.

One of our greatest needs is the enlargement of our building where out-patients are treated. This has long been an urgent want, and allusion has been made to it in the last seven consecutive annual reports. Twice a special appropriation has been asked of the City Government, and both times refused.

Last year 47,000 visits were made to these various departments by out-patients. On nearly all days the rooms are crowded; the physicians and surgeons are illy accommodated, and have not sufficient room in which to properly do their work. In many instances patients have gone away untreated, — in some instances going voluntarily, and in others sent away by the staff.

The apartments have no ventilation, and the rooms soon become foul, and in certain conditions of weather are intolerable. Several departments, for want of space, are compelled to use the same room, — in some instances contracted and encumbered with necessary apparatus for treatment, — on the same day, at different hours. This delays and obstructs the work.

The building should be twice its present size, rearranged and reconstructed. Our want is more apparent since the Massachusetts General Hospital, the Boston Dispensary, and other out-patient departments possess new and commodious rooms. An expenditure in this direction need not be large. The benefits rendered to the poor of the city would be great in comparison, and it would be sound economy, as many cases could be treated at a nominal expense, which now, by reason of this want, require admission to the hospital. The trustees and the staff are unanimous in their views upon this subject, and the trustees request me to urge of Your Honor a careful consideration of this our special need.

Our stable is in a dilapidated condition, and the poorest amongst all the departments of the city. A new structure is much needed.

The work of the present year has been free from any unusual accident, friction, or calamity. The hospital, in its various departments and services, is in efficient condition, and is doing an excellent work in the purposes for which it was founded.

I have the honor to be

Your obedient servant,

G. H. M. ROWE, M.D.,
*Superintendent and Resident Physician.*

# APPENDIX R.

OFFICE OF THE LAMP DEPARTMENT,
BOSTON, December 26, 1885.

*To His Honor* HUGH O'BRIEN,

*Mayor of the City of Boston:* —

In accordance with your request I have the honor to transmit for your consideration a statement of the financial condition of this department and its expenditures during the present municipal year, and also an account of the amount and character of the work which has been performed to date: —

The balance of appropriation from 1884 on hand
Jan. 1, 1885, was . . . . . . . . $164,951 30
Expended during the remainder of financial year
1884 and 1885 . . . . . . . . $145,953 28
Balance unexpended and transferred to other
appropriations . . . . . . . . $18,998 02
Appropriation for financial year ending April 30,
1886, was . . . . . . . . . $500,000 00
Amount expended to date . . . . . $351,125 79
Balance unexpended . . . . $148,874 21

An amount sufficient to meet all anticipated expenditures of the department during the remainder of the present financial year.

The cost of gas for street-lighting during the year
ending Dec. 15, 1884, was . $255,463 30

The cost of gas for street-lighting during the year
ending Dec. 15, 1885, was . . . . $255,059 59

Decrease during present year . . . . $403 71

Cost of oil for street-lighting during the year
ending Dec. 15, 1884, was . . . . $5,566 83

Cost of oil for street-lighting during the year
ending Dec. 15, 1885, was . $5,141 63

Decrease during present year . . . . $425 20

Cost of electric lighting during year ending Dec. 15,
1884, was . . . . . . . . $90,785 80

Cost of electric lighting during year ending Dec. 15,
1885, was . . . . . . . . $99,523 28

Increase during present year . . . . $8,737 48

Cost of lighting and care of street-lights during
year ending Dec. 15, 1884, was . . . $102,390 84

Cost of lighting and care of street-lights during
year ending Dec. 15, 1885, was . . . $103,074 32

Increase during present year . . . . $683 48

Total expenditure for all purposes during year
ending Dec. 15, 1884 . . . . . $491,653 16

Total expenditures for all purposes during year
ending Dec. 15, 1885 . . . . . $497,080 22

Increase during present year . $5,427 06


The number of lamps in the city on Jan. 1, 1885,
was, viz. : —

Gas                    .              .  9,781
Oil            .            .         .  2,591
Large gas lamps                       .     36
Electric lights  .   .                     401
                                        _____
    Total number Jan. 1, 1885            12,809

The number of lamps in the city January 1, 1886, is, viz. : —

| | |
|---|---:|
| Gas . . . . | 9,978 |
| Oil . . . . . | 2,630 |
| Large gas lamps . . . . | 63 |
| Electric lights . . . . | 443 |
| Total number, January 1, 1886 . . | 13,114 |

The increase during the year was : —

| | |
|---|---:|
| Gas . . . . . . | 197 |
| Oil . . . . | 39 |
| Large gas lamps . . | 27 |
| Electric lights . . | 42 |
| Total increase during year 1885 . . . | 305 |

The number of new lights added during the year 1885, was, viz. : —

| | |
|---|---:|
| Gas . . . . . . . . . | 215 |
| Oil · . . . . . . . | 85 |
| Large gas lamps . . . . . . | 28 |
| Electric lights . . . . . . | 43 |
| Total number added during 1885 . | 371 |
| "            "      1884 . | 186 |
| Increase over last year . . | 185 |

During the year 80 lights have been discontinued, from various causes, principally the introduction of electric lights, and a large number of oil lamps in the outlying districts have been changed to gas.

The petitions for lights of all kinds, during the present

year have been unusually numerous, and persistently urged, and in response to the public demand the number of lamps has been been largely increased, although the appropriation remains the same as it has been for three years, viz., $500,000.

Should the same amount of work be done next year, and should a liberal spirit be shown in regard to electric lighting, it will be necessary, in order to provide for the increased expenditures, that the appropriation for this department should be increased to at least $550,000.

Respectfully submitted,

HUGH J. TOLAND,
*Superintendent of Lamps.*

---

# APPENDIX S.

---

DEPARTMENT OF COMMON AND SQUARES, CITY HALL,
BOSTON, December 28, 1885.

*To His Honor* MAYOR O'BRIEN : —

DEAR SIR, — In obedience to your request I beg to submit for your consideration a synopsis of the condition of the Department of Common and Public Grounds at the present time, together with its principal wants and requirements for the ensuing year.

The improvements that have been made during the past year on the Common, Public Garden, Commonwealth avenue, Blackstone and Franklin squares, East and West Chester park, etc., are so well known and so fully appreciated by the public that I deem it unnecessary to enlarge upon their improved condition.

For years past the development of the department has been circumscribed, and to a degree crippled, for want of suitable quarters for its natural growth. During a long period we have been compelled to pay for the temporary use of greenhouses from twelve to fourteen hundred ($1,200 to $1,400) dollars per year, and for the partial storage of settees, tools, etc., seven hundred and twenty ($720) dollars per year, besides being obliged to mar one of the most sightly and interesting portions of the Common by the storage of hundreds of thousands of plants, that are indispensable for the ornamentation of the public grounds.

As a relief from this dilemma, and as an illustration of their wisdom, the City Government voted us $2\frac{2}{3}$ acres of land, known as the Roxbury Canal land; and also twenty-five hundred ($2,500) dollars for its improvement. With this amount I have built a substantial and ample storehouse, $246' \times 30'$, for the sum of fourteen hundred and forty-one and $\frac{50}{100}$ ($1,441\frac{50}{100}$) dollars; and have also surrounded the whole area with a matched-board pine fence 1,496 feet long by 8 feet high, for nine hundred and twenty ($920) dollars. Thus it will be seen that the rent of a partial storage for two years covered the cost of the new building. It may also prove of interest to state that the highest estimate for the work of the building and fence was forty-nine hundred and twenty-one ($4,921) dollars, — a difference of twenty-five hundred and fifty-nine and $\frac{50}{100}$ ($2,559\frac{50}{100}$) dollars between the highest and lowest bids.

The extra requirements of the department for the ensuing year will be the erection of suitable but inexpensive greenhouses and frames upon the newly acquired land; the immediate removal in the early spring of all the unsightly encumbrances from the Deer park on the Common, and its speedy transformation into a grassy sward; the renovation of the five lower sections of Commonwealth avenue, between West Chester park and Dartmouth street, in the same manner as we improved East and West Chester park. A similar treatment should be given to all the parks in East Boston, to enable them to grow healthy trees or grass.

The iron fence surrounding Independence square has been in a dilapidated condition for years, and should be either removed or put in proper repair.

The shade-trees upon our public streets, which have been neglected for the past four years for want of funds, should receive immediate attention, and a liberal appropriation should be made next year to place them in a condition satisfactory to real-estate owners and the tax-payers in general.

I beg to call particular attention to the necessity of employing a Special Police force for the protection of the property of this department.

With these and a few other minor improvements the department will be in a healthy, progressive, working condition, and must prove to the citizens of Boston a source of pleasure and delight.

I remain, your obedient servant,

WM. DOOGUE,<br>*Superintendent.*